4th

Social Studies

Daily Practice Workbook
20 weeks of fun activities

ARGOPREP

 History •  Civics and Government •  Geography •  Economics

ArgoPrep is one of the leading providers of supplemental educational products and services. We offer affordable and effective test prep solutions to educators, parents and students. Learning should be fun and easy! To access more resources visit us at www.argoprep.com.

Our goal is to make your life easier, so let us know how we can help you by e-mailing us at: info@argoprep.com.

- ArgoPrep is a recipient of the prestigious **Mom's Choice Award**.
- ArgoPrep also received the 2019 **Seal of Approval** from Homeschool.com for our award-winning workbooks.
- ArgoPrep was awarded the 2019 **National Parenting Products Award, Gold Medal Parent's Choice Award** and **the Tillywig Brain Child Award.**

SOCIAL STUDIES

Social Studies Daily Practice Workbook by ArgoPrep allows students to build foundational skills and review concepts. Our workbooks explore social studies topics in depth with ArgoPrep's 5 E's to build social studies mastery.

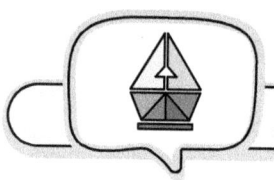
Introduction

Welcome to our fourth grade social studies workbook!

This workbook has been specifically designed to help students build mastery of foundational social studies skills that are taught in fourth grade. Included are 20 weeks of comprehensive instruction covering the four branches of social studies: Geography, History, Civics and Government, and Economics.

This workbook dedicates five weeks of instruction to each of the four branches of social studies, focusing on different standards within each week of instruction.

Within the branch of Geography, students will learn about the world community and understand topics such as maps and models. Students will take a deep dive specifically into New York geography and learn fundamental concepts. The second branch is History, where students will learn about european explorers, the French & Indian War, and the Revolutionary War. In Civics and Government, they will learn more about the three branches of government as well as human rights. Finally, in the Economics section, students will have the opportunity to learn about industrialization, transportation, and immigration.

At the conclusion of the 20 weeks of instruction, students should have a solid grasp of the concepts required by the National Council for Social Studies for fourth grade.

Table of Contents

How to Use the Book

All 20 weeks of daily activity pages in this book follow the same weekly structure. The book is divided into four sections: Geography, History, Civics and Government, and Economics. The activities in each of the sections align to the recommendations of the National Council for the Social Studies which will help prepare students for state standardized assessments. While the sections can be completed in any order, it is important to complete each week within the section in chronological order since the skills often build upon one another.

Each week focuses on one specific topic within the section. More information about the weekly structure can be found in the Weekly Planner section.

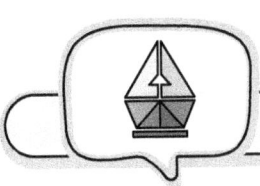
Weekly Planner

Day	Activity	Description
1	Engaging with the Topic	Read a short text on the topic and answer multiple choice questions.
2	Exploring the Topic	Interact with the topic on a deeper level by collecting, analyzing, and interpreting information.
3	Explaining the Topic	Make sense of the topic by explaining and beginning to draw conclusions about information.
4	Experiencing the Topic	Investigate the topic by making real-life connections.
5	Elaborating on the Topic	Reflect on the topic and use all information learned to draw conclusions and evaluate results.

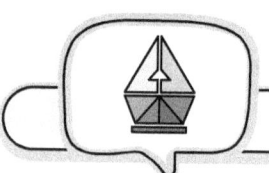
List of Topics

How to access video explanations?

Go to **argoprep.com/social4**
OR scan the QR Code:

WEEK 1

Geography

Where is New York Located?

New York

Discover the state of New York using geography tools such as maps.

Directions: Read the text below. Then answer the questions that follow.

Welcome to **New York!** This Northeastern state, also known as the Empire State, has a rich history due to its location and **geography**. New York State can be described as a location within the Northern and Western hemispheres on the continent of North America. It is one of the fifty states in the United States of America. With over 19 million people, New York has the fourth largest state **population** in the country. Close to 8.5 million of the state's residents live in New York City, the largest and most well-known city in the state.

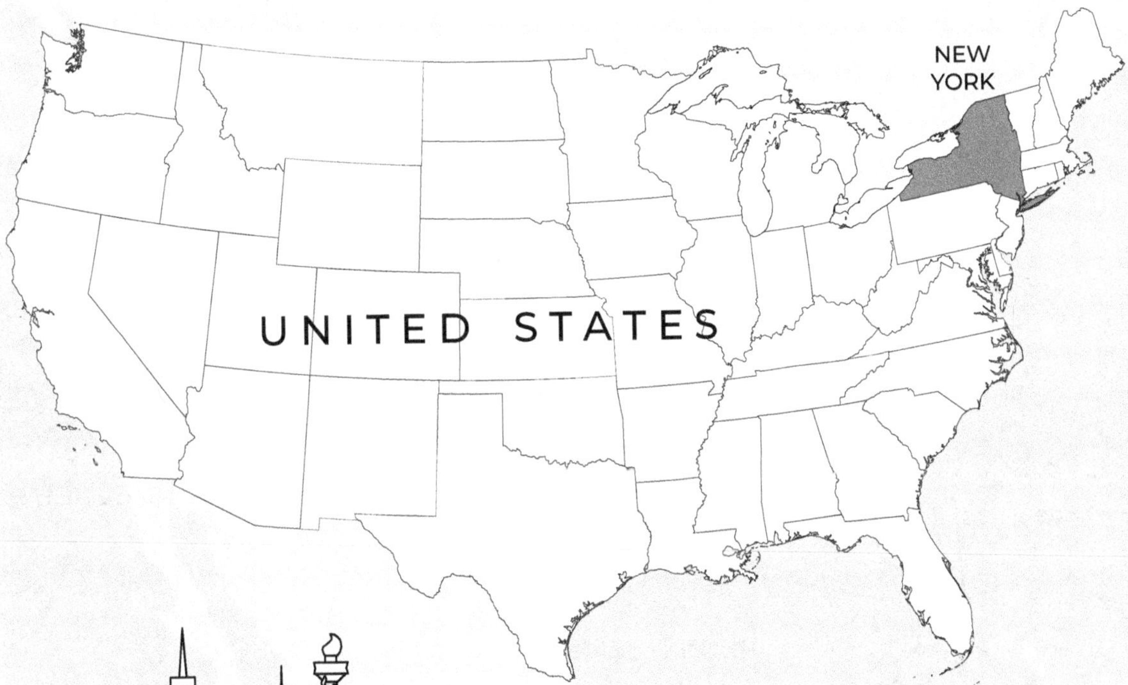

NEW YORK

UNITED STATES

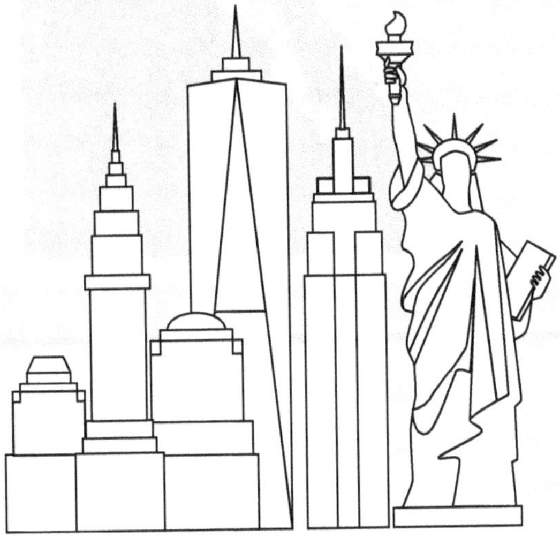

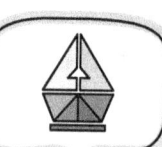
"

   Maps can be used to examine the geography of New York State and other places around the world. Different maps are used for different purposes. A **political map** shows the borders, boundaries, and names of countries, states, counties, and cities. Many times, political maps use different colors to make them easier to read. Most physical features, such as mountains, are not included on political maps. As you can see from the map below, New York is bordered by Vermont, Connecticut, Massachusetts, Pennsylvania, New Jersey, and the country of Canada.

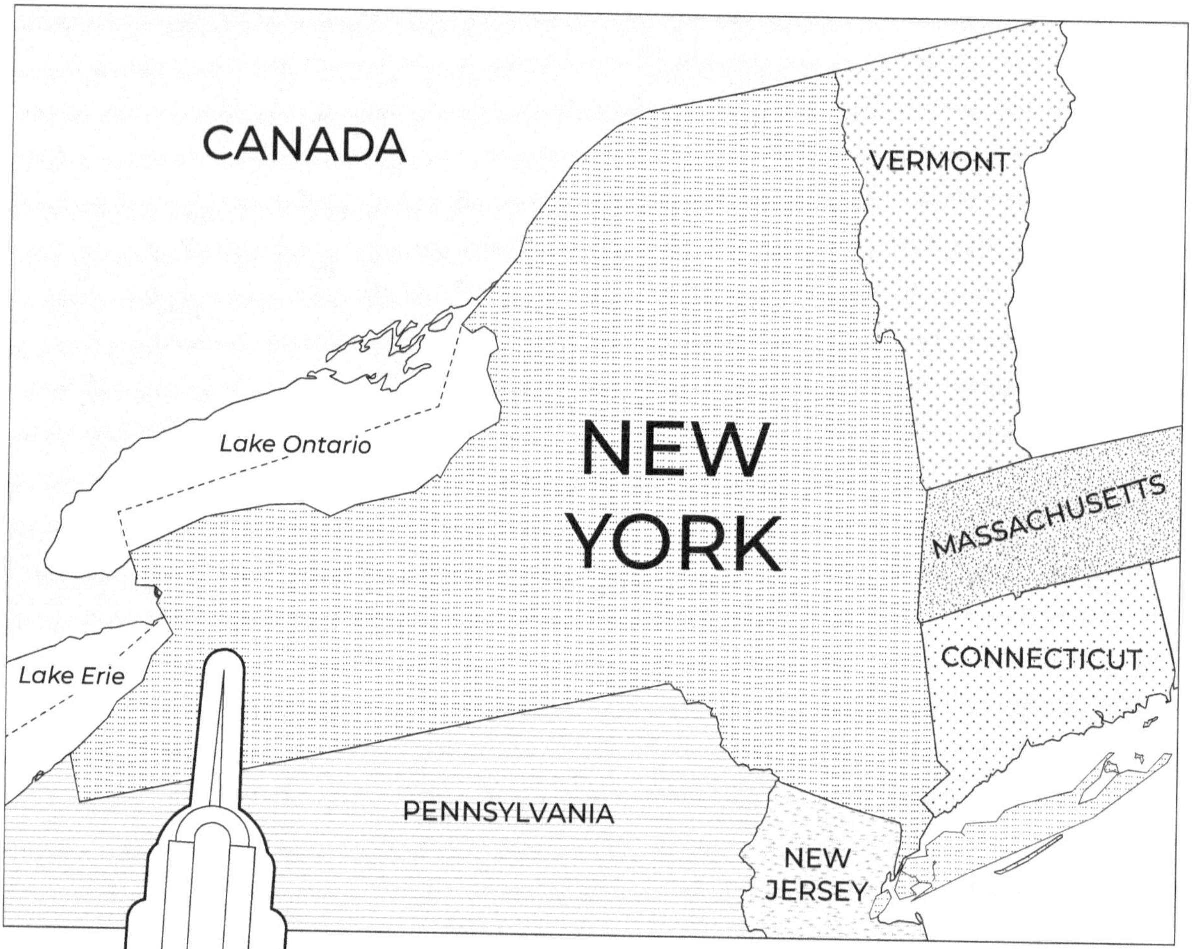

CANADA

VERMONT

Lake Ontario

NEW
YORK

MASSACHUSETTS

CONNECTICUT

Lake Erie

PENNSYLVANIA

NEW
JERSEY

"

NEW
YORK

1. Describe where in the world the state of New York is located.

2. What is geography?

    A. the process of finding a state on a map

    B. the study of people and places on Earth

    C. an important part of a state's history

    D. a group of people who live together in a location

3. What is a political map?

    A. a map that shows where landforms in a region are located

    B. a map that shows only the coordinates of a certain location

    C. a map that shows the borders and names of countries, states, and cities

    D. a map that is used to show pilots the best flight pattern to follow

4. What is the population of the state of New York?

    A. about 8.5 million people

    B. close to 4 million people

    C. over 19 million people

    D. the highest population in the country

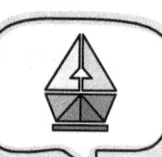
Directions: Read the text below. Then answer the questions that follow.

Yesterday you learned about political maps. They can give lots of information about a location. However, we often use **relative location** when describing where something is located. Relative location is used to describe the location of a place in relation to other places. For example, how would you describe to a friend or family member where your classroom is located in relation to the cafeteria or the library? You probably would not pull out a political map. You would use words such as "next to" or "on the right of." This is called giving the relative location.

The cardinal and intermediate directions on a **compass rose** can help you describe the relative location of a certain place on a map. As you can see from the map below, New York State is located Northeast of Texas and West of Massachusetts.

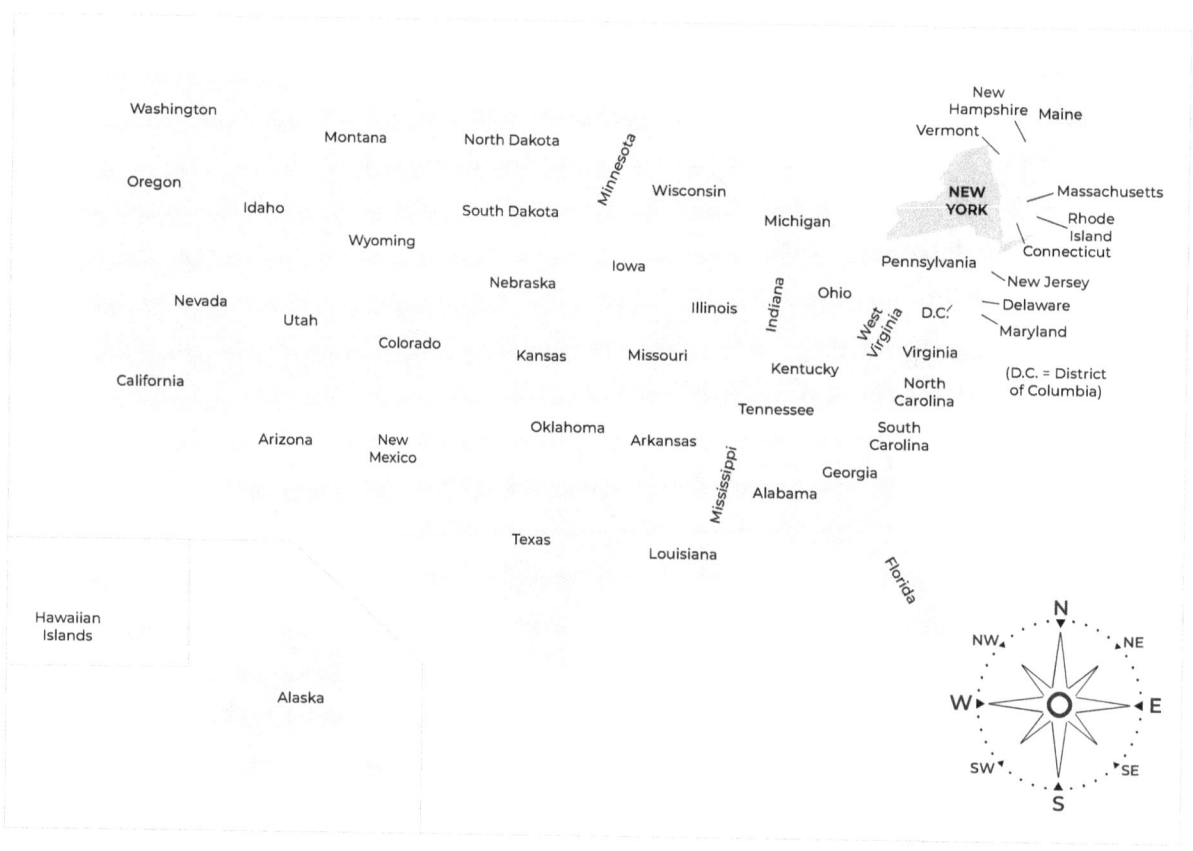

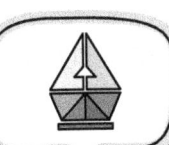
If you were an airline pilot, you would need to be more specific with location. A more accurate way to describe the location of a place on a map is to use the lines of **latitude** and **longitude.** Lines of latitude run east to west and lines of longitude run north to south. Together, they create an imaginary grid pattern, as you can see below, that covers our planet. This system, which is measured in **degrees** (°), can pinpoint any exact location on Earth.

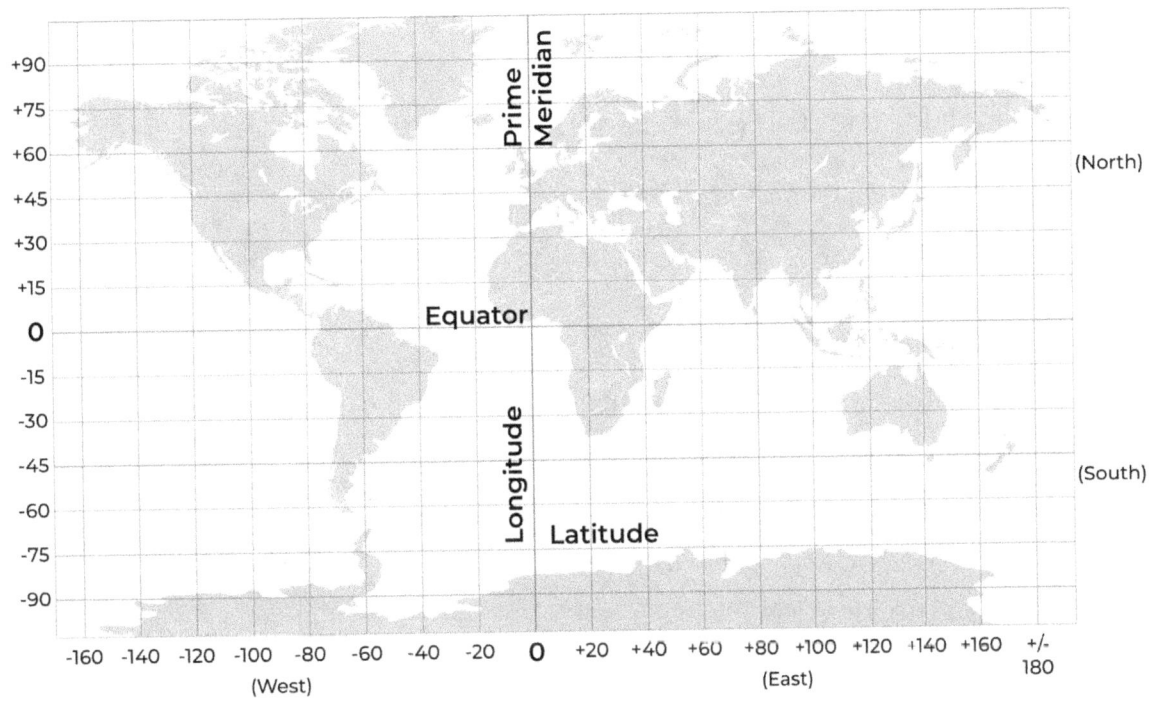

The equator is a line of latitude located at 0°. The prime meridian is a line of longitude located at 0°. To find a location's **coordinates** you simply see where the lines of latitude and longitude **intersect** or meet. For example, Washington, D.C.'s coordinates are 39° N, 77° W.

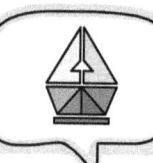
1. When you describe a location in relation to something else, you are using...

2. What can be found on a compass rose? Select all that apply.

   A. intermediate directions

   B. a political map

   C. cardinal directions

   D. degrees

3. The imaginary lines that run north to south on Earth are called

   A. lines of latitude

   B. the equator

   C. a compass rose

   D. lines of longitude

4. When lines of latitude and longitude intersect, what can they tell us about a location?

   A. the population of the location

   B. the coordinates of the location

   C. the border or boundary of the location

   D. the capital of the location

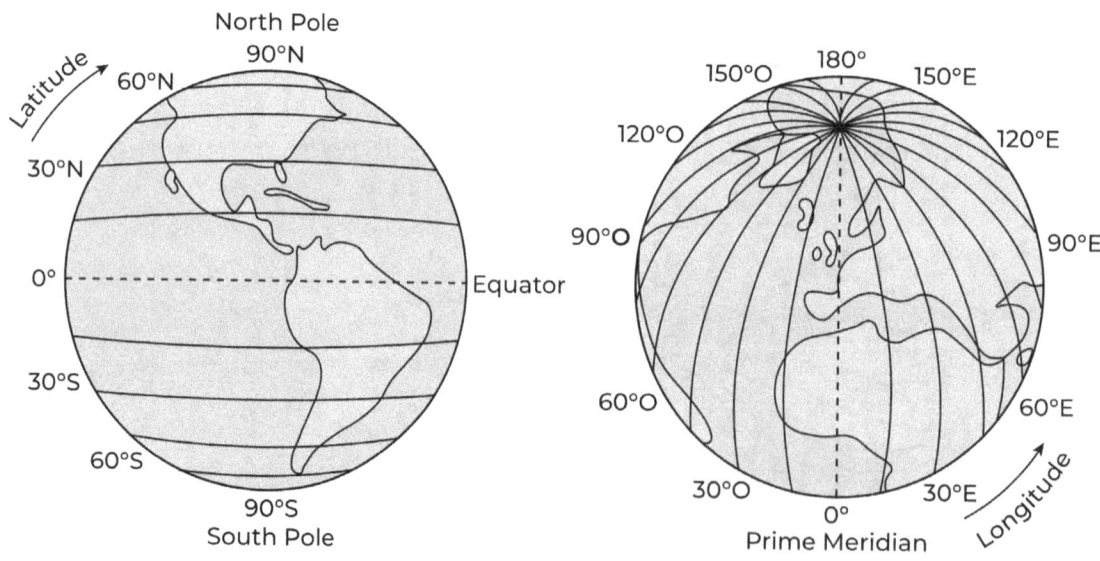

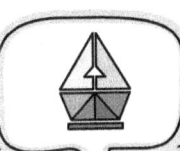
Directions: Read the text below. Then answer the questions that follow.

You have learned that a political map shows the borders of states and the location of cities. It will not show the physical characteristics of the land such as mountains. The **capital** city of New York is **Albany**. Find Albany on the map below and place a star next to it. The five largest cities in New York are New York City, Buffalo, Rochester, Yonkers, and Syracuse. Place a box around each of these largely populated cities. Do you live in New York? Is your home city located on this map? If it is, circle it.

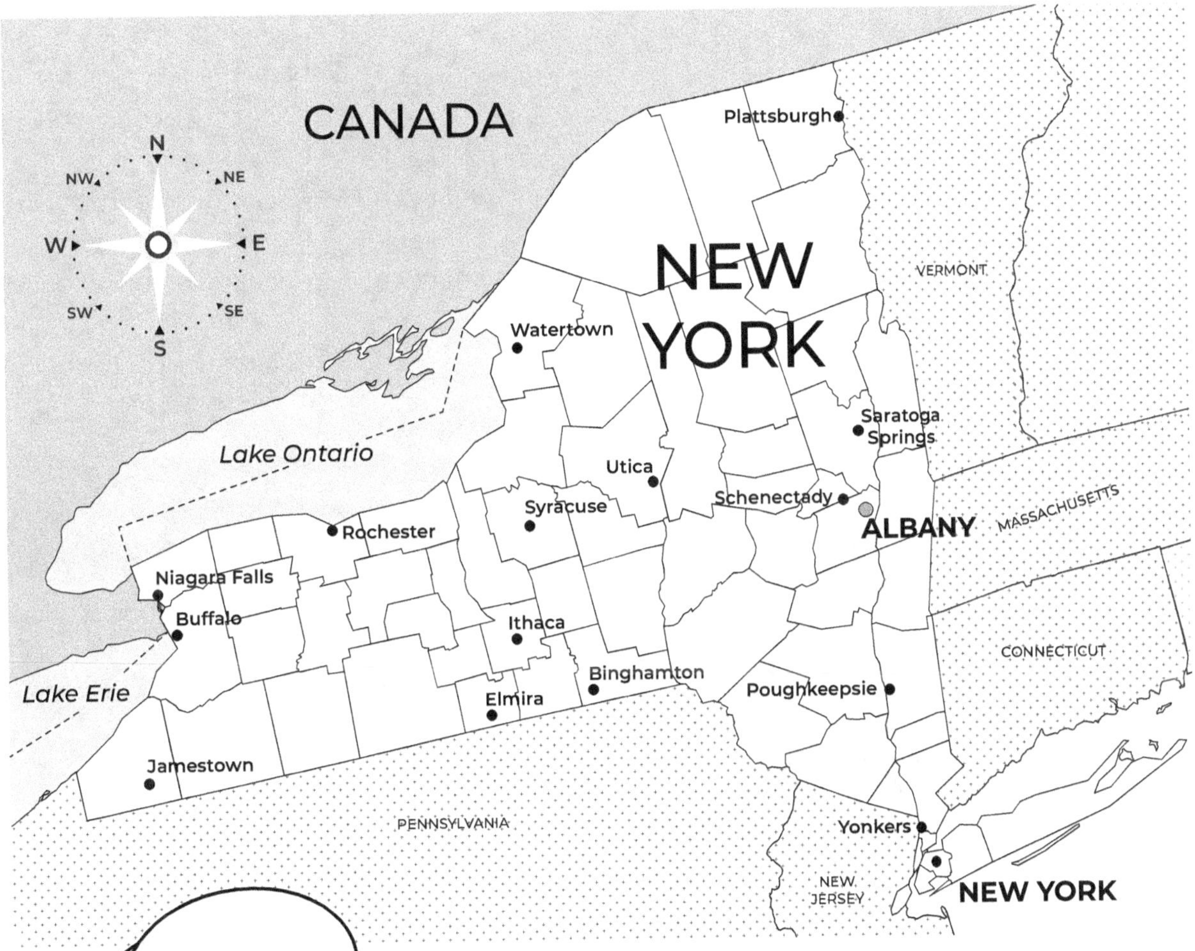

CANADA

N
NW   NE
W   O   E
SW   SE
S

Plattsburgh

NEW YORK

VERMONT

Watertown

Lake Ontario

Saratoga Springs

Utica

Syracuse

Schenectady

Rochester

ALBANY

MASSACHUSETTS

Niagara Falls

Buffalo

Ithaca

Lake Erie

Binghamton

Poughkeepsie

CONNECTICUT

Elmira

Jamestown

PENNSYLVANIA

Yonkers

NEW JERSEY

NEW YORK

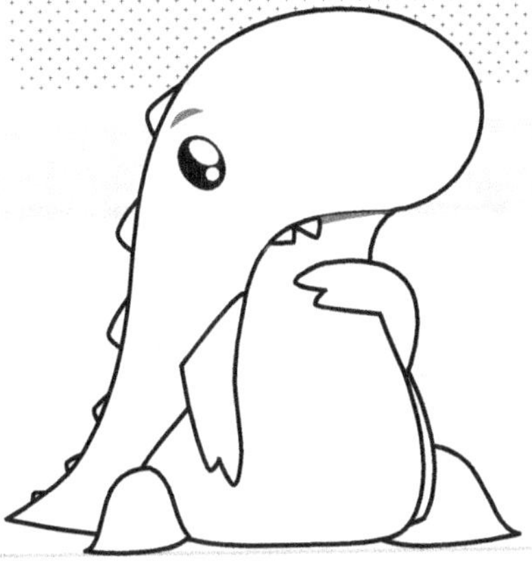

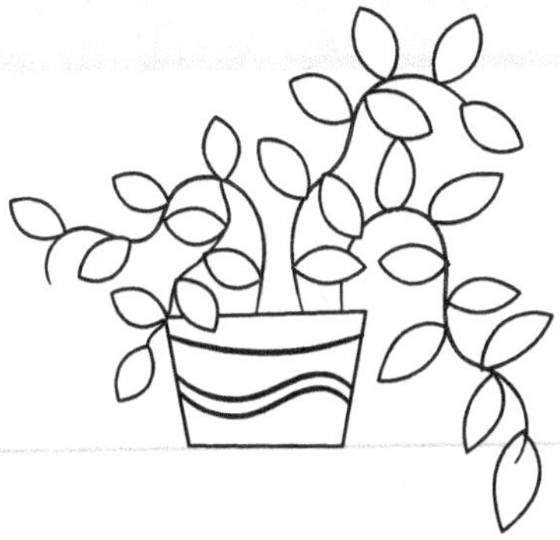

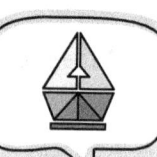
"

Remember that location can be described in a variety of ways. **Relative location** is used to describe the location of a place in relation to other places, while the **coordinate location** is used to give an exact location.

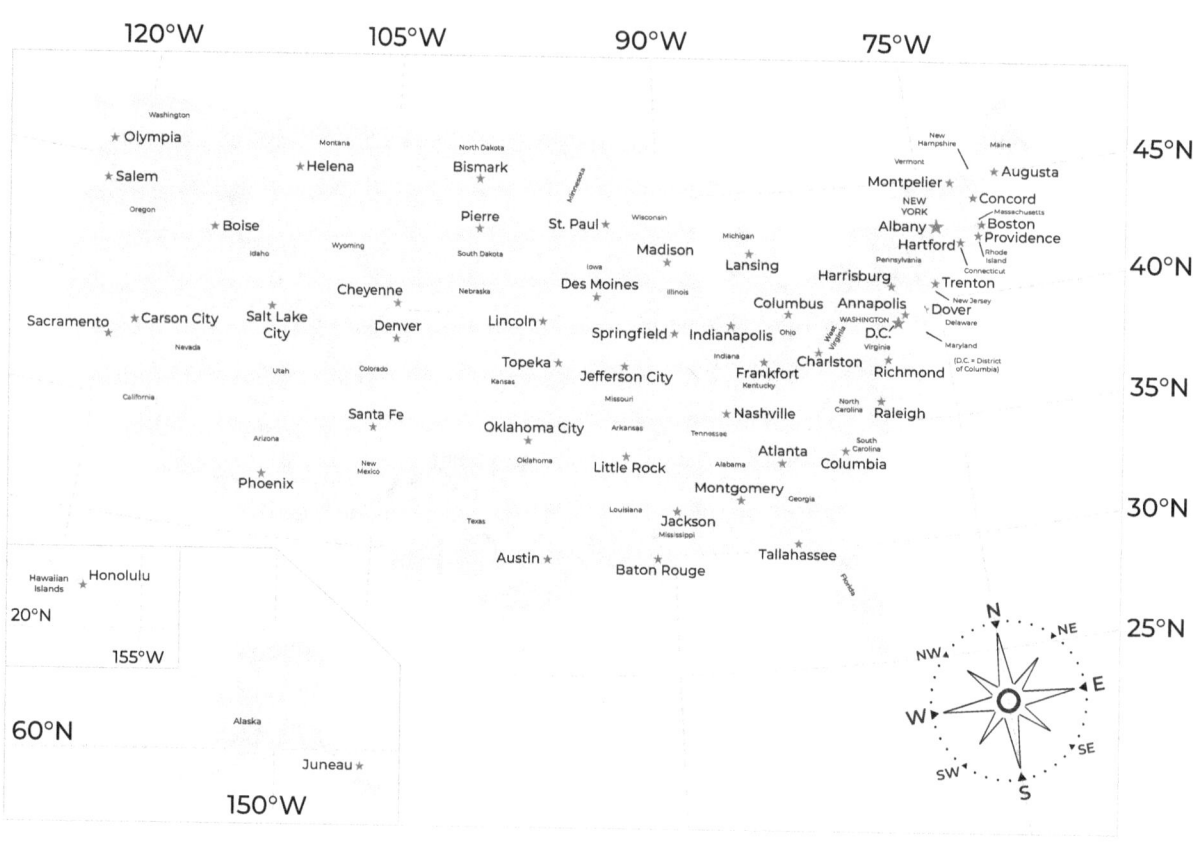

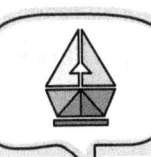
Find New York State on the latitude and longitude map of the United States on page 16. Place a star in the middle of the state. You can estimate that New York is located at 45°N, 76°W.

1. What is the capital city of New York?

   A. New York City

   B. Buffalo

   C. Syracuse

   D. Albany

2. Using the compass rose, give the relative location of each of these cities. Look at the political map of New York on page 15 to help you.

   A. Jamestown is .... of Elmira.

   B. Albany is .... of Watertown.

   C. Syracuse is .... of Poughkeepsie.

   D. Utica is .... of Ithaca.

3. Explain the main difference between relative and coordinate location.

4. What is the estimate of the coordinate location of New York's capital city?

   A. 40°N, 50°W

   B. 43°N, 74°W

   C. 45°S, 76°E

   D. 40°S, 74°W

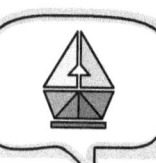
Directions: Read the text below. Then answer the questions that follow.

You know that political maps can give important information about the location of a certain place. Create a political map of New York State. You must include and label the capital city, the five most populated cities, your own community (if you live in New York), and the bordering states.

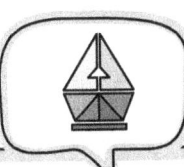
This week you learned about the location of New York in relation to the rest of the world. You also learned about political maps and how to describe a location using both relative and exact directions.

Directions: Read the text below. Then answer the questions that follow.

1. Think of an occupation that relies on the use of political maps. What occupation is it and why are political maps necessary for their job description?

....

....

2. Complete the Venn diagram to compare and contrast relative and coordinate location.

Relative   **Coordinate**

3. Look back at the map of New York and the location of the five most populated cities. What do you notice about all five of these cities and their location within the state of New York? Make some predictions about why you think those five cities are so heavily populated.

....

....

....

Geography

New York Geography

Explore physical features, climate, and agriculture in New York.

ARGOPREP

Directions: Read the text below. Then answer the questions that follow.

New York State has a variety of **physical features** including rivers, oceans, waterfalls, lakes, forests, valleys, and mountains. Anyone traveling across this **diverse** state is sure to discover many unique landforms, such as the Atlantic Ocean, Niagara Falls, and the Adirondack Mountains.

A **physical map** shows the physical features of a location. People use physical maps to locate **landforms** such as mountains, rivers, and valleys. Sometimes physical maps will show major **political boundaries** such as countries or states. This helps the person reading the map know where the physical features are located. Physical maps also use different colors. These are used to show the different **elevations** (height) of Earth's natural landscape.

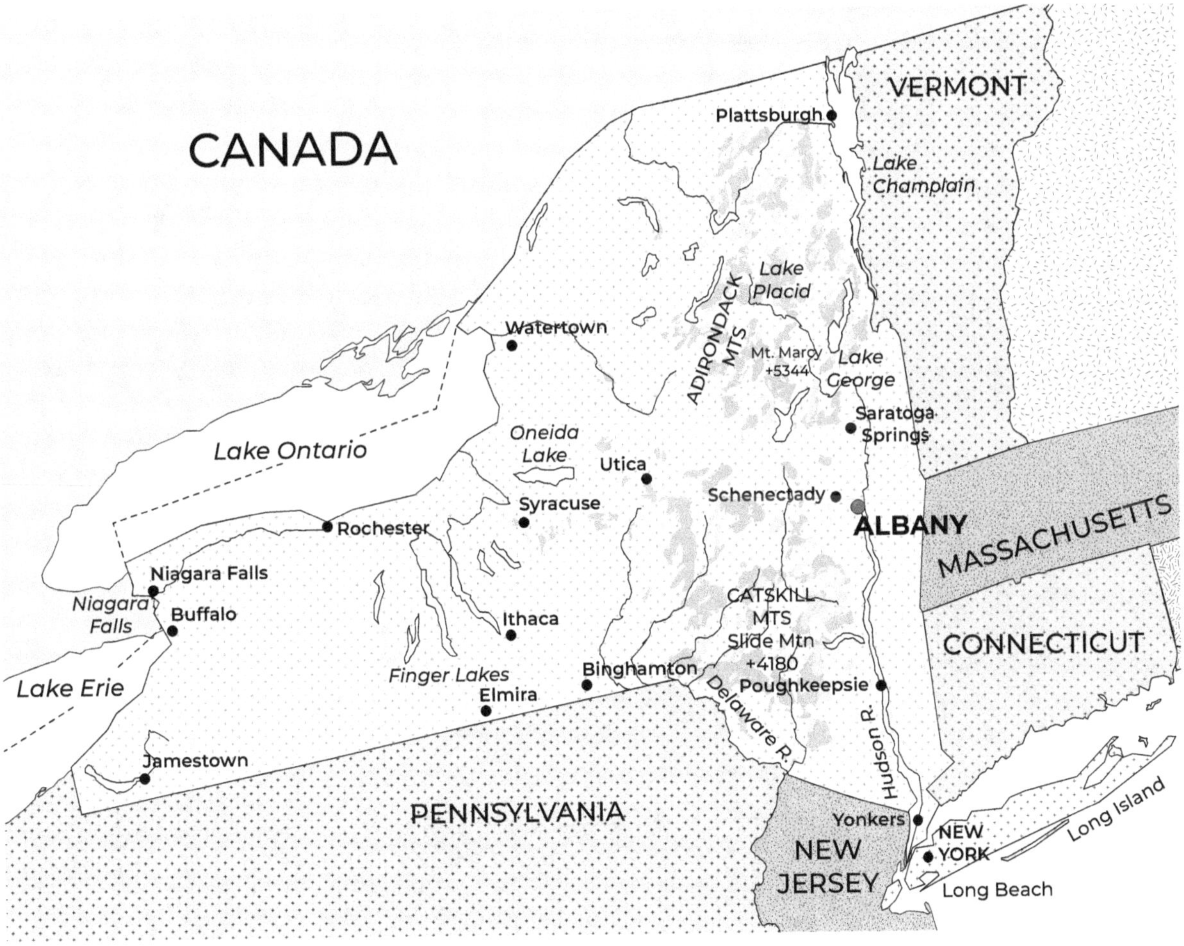

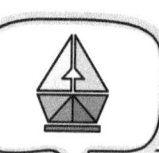
1. What can be found on a physical map? Select all that apply.

    A. mountains
    B. street names
    C. rivers
    D. population
    E. rainfall totals
    F. valleys

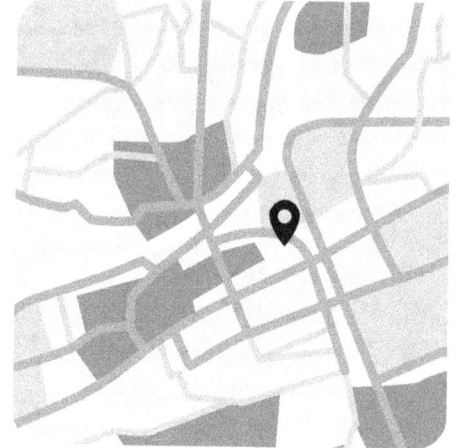

2. What is elevation?

    A. distance
    B. color
    C. direction
    D. height

3. What feature helps people read physical maps?

    A. elevation
    B. color
    C. scale
    D. title

4. What makes New York geography diverse?

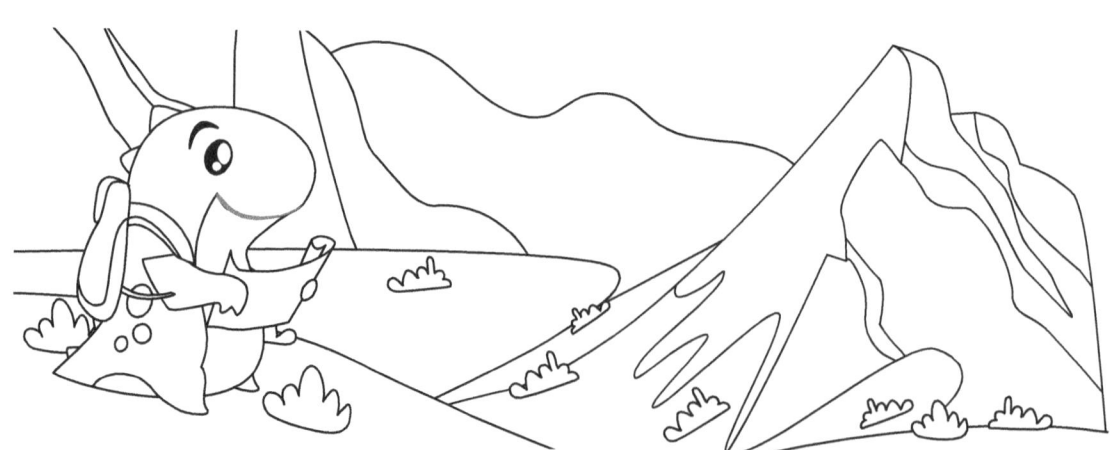

Directions: Read the text below. Then answer the questions that follow.

Yesterday you learned about physical maps. Analyze the map below to find the following landforms on the map:

1. Lake Ontario
2. Finger Lakes
3. Catskill Mountains
4. Long Island
5. Adirondack Mountains
6. Delaware River
7. Niagara Falls
8. Long Beach
9. Lake Placid

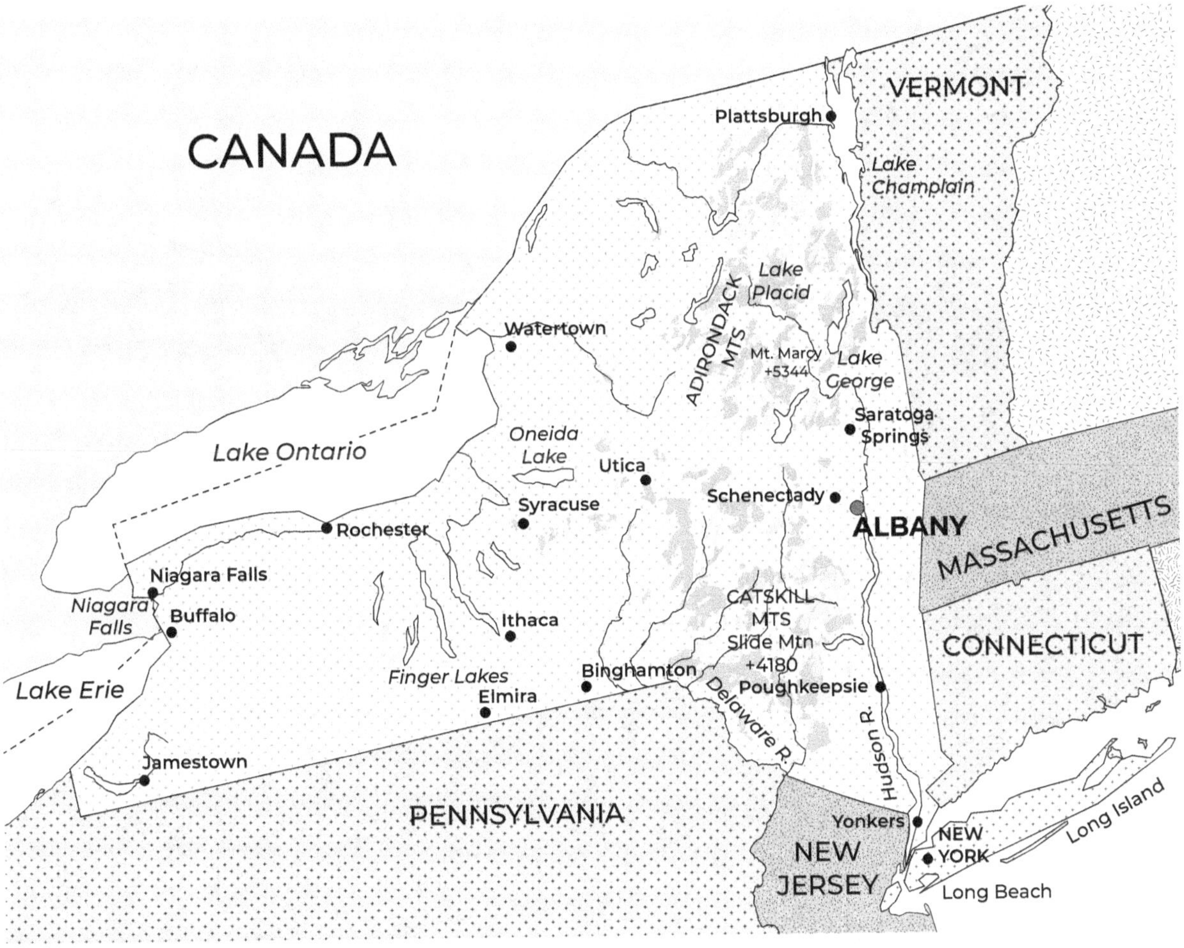

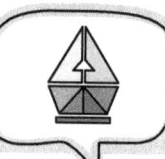
1. List 2 landforms in New York. Where are they located?

   A.

   B.

2. What country borders New York?

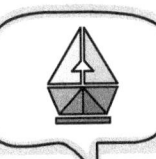
Directions: Read the text below. Then answer the questions that follow.

This is a **Plant Hardiness Map** of New York. The colors show the **annual minimum temperature** in each geographic area. People in agriculture use this map to determine when it is safe to plant certain things outside. In areas with a mild climate, the growing season is longer. If areas tend to have a colder climate, they will have shorter growing seasons.

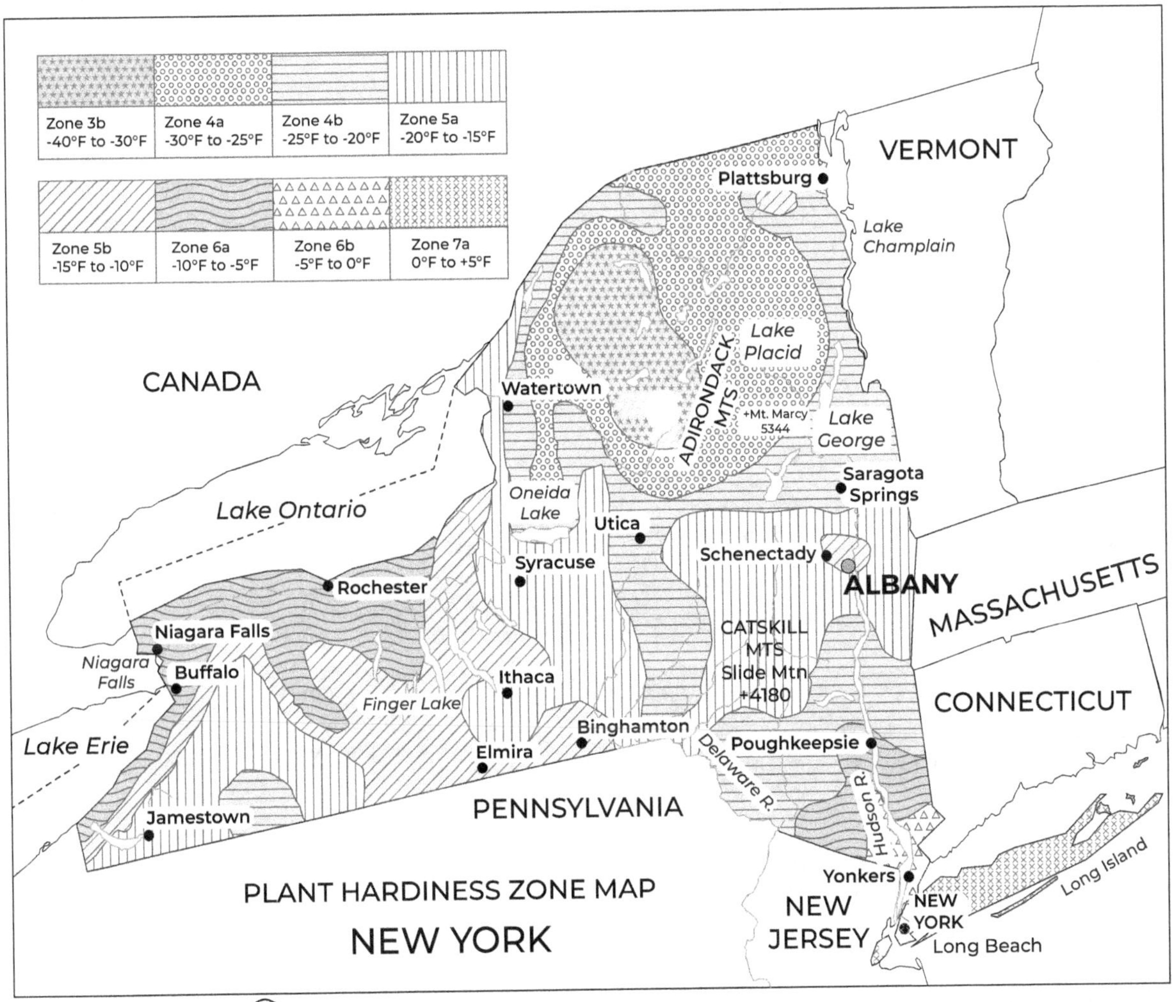

Zone 3b -40°F to -30°F	Zone 4a -30°F to -25°F	Zone 4b -25°F to -20°F	Zone 5a -20°F to -15°F
Zone 5b -15°F to -10°F	Zone 6a -10°F to -5°F	Zone 6b -5°F to 0°F	Zone 7a 0°F to +5°F

VERMONT

Plattsburg •

Lake Champlain

CANADA

Lake Placid

ADIRONDACK MTS

Watertown

+Mt. Marcy 5344

Lake George

Lake Ontario

Oneida Lake

Saragota • Springs

Utica •

Syracuse •

Schenectady •

MASSACHUSETTS

• Rochester

ALBANY

Niagara Falls

CATSKILL MTS Slide Mtn +4180

CONNECTICUT

Niagara Falls

Buffalo •

Ithaca •

Lake Erie

Finger Lake

Binghamton •

Poughkeepsie •

Elmira •

Delaware R.

Hudson R.

Long Island

• Jamestown

PENNSYLVANIA

Yonkers •

PLANT HARDINESS ZONE MAP

NEW YORK

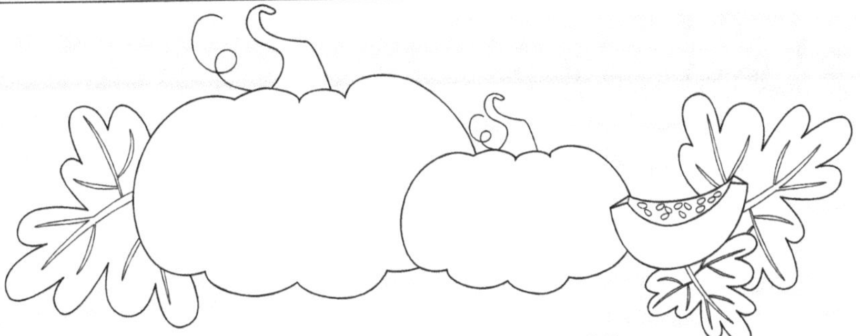

NEW JERSEY

NEW YORK

Long Beach

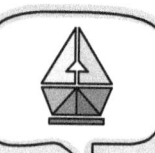
" Landforms can affect an area's **climate.** For example, large bodies of water, such as lakes, can keep areas cooler in the summer and warmer in the winter. Therefore, it can be helpful to use a physical map to help you analyze an **agricultural map.**

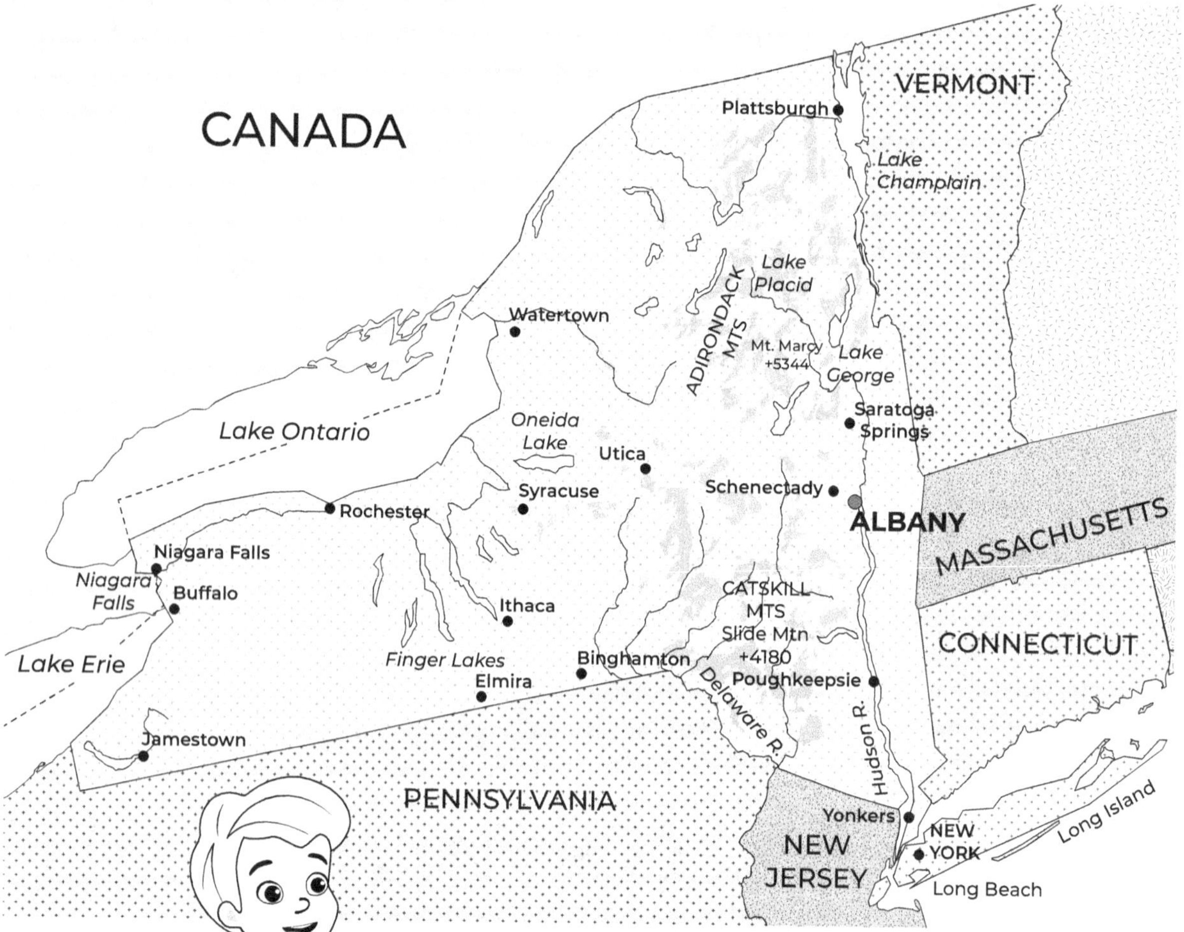

CANADA

VERMONT

Plattsburgh

Lake Champlain

Lake Placid

Watertown

ADIRONDACK MTS

Mt. Marcy +5344

Lake George

Saratoga Springs

Oneida Lake

Lake Ontario

Utica

Syracuse

Rochester

Schenectady

ALBANY

MASSACHUSETTS

Niagara Falls

Niagara Falls

Buffalo

Ithaca

CATSKILL MTS
Slide Mtn +4180

CONNECTICUT

Lake Erie

Finger Lakes

Elmira

Binghamton

Poughkeepsie

Delaware R.

Hudson R.

Jamestown

PENNSYLVANIA

Yonkers

NEW YORK

NEW JERSEY

Long Island

Long Beach

"

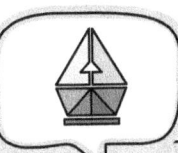
North Country

Mohawk Valley

Finger Lakes

Western New York

Capital District

Hudson Valley

Central New York

Southern Tier

Long Island

CLINTON
FRANKLIN
ST. LAWRENCE
ESSEX
JEFFERSON
HAMILTON
LEWIS
HERKIMER
WARREN
WASHINGTON
SARATOGA
OSWEGO
ONEIDA
FULTON
SCHENEC-TADY
MONT-GOMERY
RENSSELAER
ALBANY ★
ALBANY
ORLEANS
MONROE
WAYNE
ONONDAGA
MADISON
SCHOHARIE
COLUMBIA
GREENE
NIAGARA
GENESEE
ONTARIO
SENECA
CAYUGA
CORTLAND
CHENANGO
OSTEGO
DUTCHESS
ERIE
WYOMING
LIVINGSTON
YATES
TOMPKINS
DELAWARE
ULSTER
SCHUY-LER
STEUBEN
CHE-MUNG
TIOGA
BROOME
SULLIVAN
ALLEGANY
CATTARAUGUS
PUTNAM
CHAUTAUQUA
ORANGE
WEST-CHESTER
SUFFOLK
ROCKLAND
BRONX
NASSAU
NEW YORK
NEW YORK
RICHMOND
QUEENS
KINGS

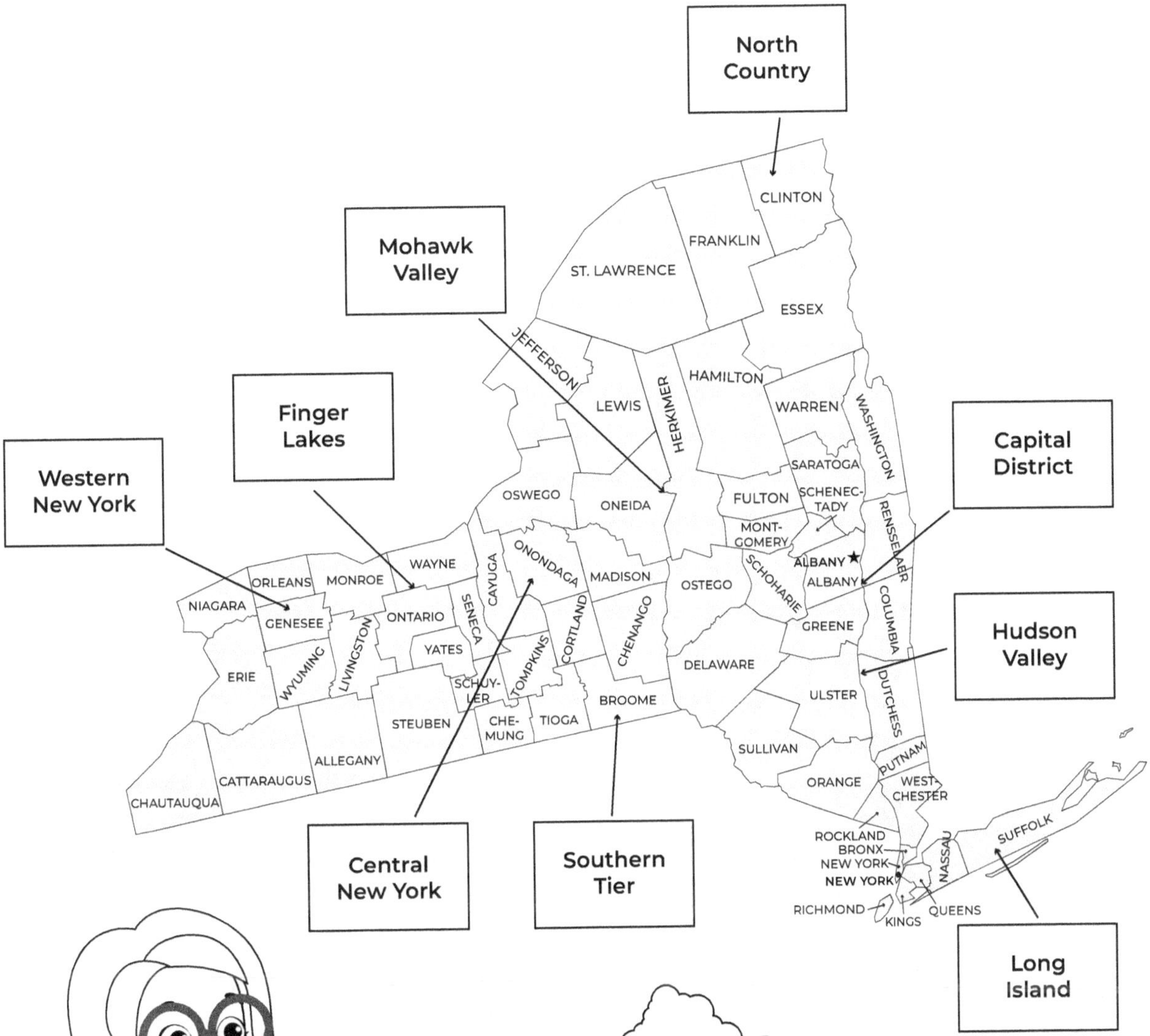

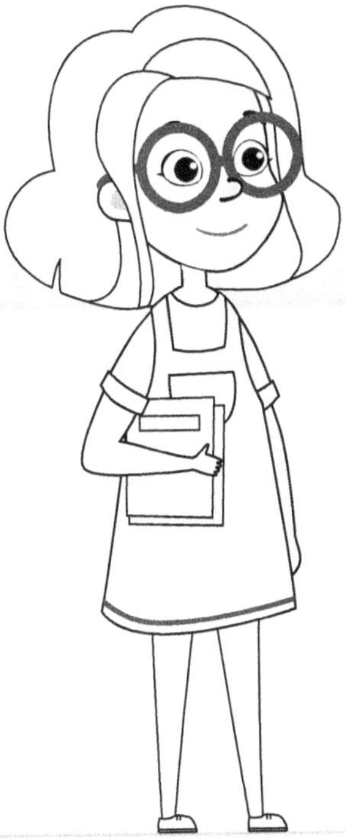

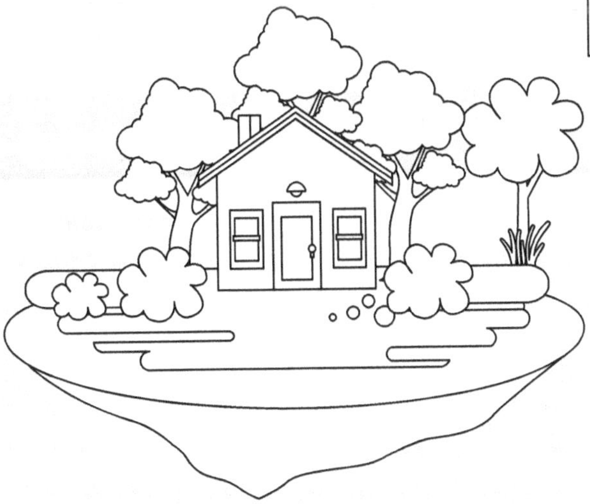

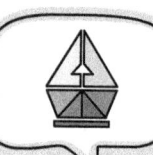
1. Name one area of New York that has a milder climate. (Use the map on page 25 and 27 to help you answer the questions on this page.)

2. Name one area of New York that has a colder climate.

3. How can a physical map help you analyze an agricultural map?

Directions: Read the text below. Then answer the questions that follow.

You have learned about how climate and physical features can affect the way people live in New York. Which region would you prefer to live in? Explain how factors such as physical features, climate, agriculture, etc. make this region a good place for people to live. You can use the map on page 25 and 27 to help you select a region.

Region	Physical Features	Climate	Explanation

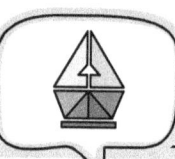
This week you learned about the geography of New York. Using a physical map, you found New York's most popular landforms. You also learned how to read a thematic map (Plant Hardiness Map). Using different types of maps, you experienced how to find information about a specific region or area.

Directions: Read the text below. Then answer the questions that follow.

1. What makes the physical features of New York diverse?

....

....

....

2. Explain how maps are important for farmers.

....

....

....

3. What is the relationship between the physical features and climate of an area?

....

....

....

....

WEEK 3

Geography

The First New Yorkers

Learn about Native American groups as the first inhabitants of New York.

ARGOPREP

Directions: Read the text below. Then answer the questions that follow.

Native American groups, primarily the Haudenosaunee (Iroquois) and Algonquian-speaking groups, were the first people to live in the area that is now New York State. They relied on the environment for survival. They used **natural resources** for food, clothing, and shelter. Therefore, the geography of the land determined where they settled down.

You learned that the region where New York is located is very diverse. There are numerous mountains, valleys, lakes, rivers, and oceans that Native American groups would find useful. Are you located on the map below? What physical features are near you that would have been useful to the first New Yorkers?

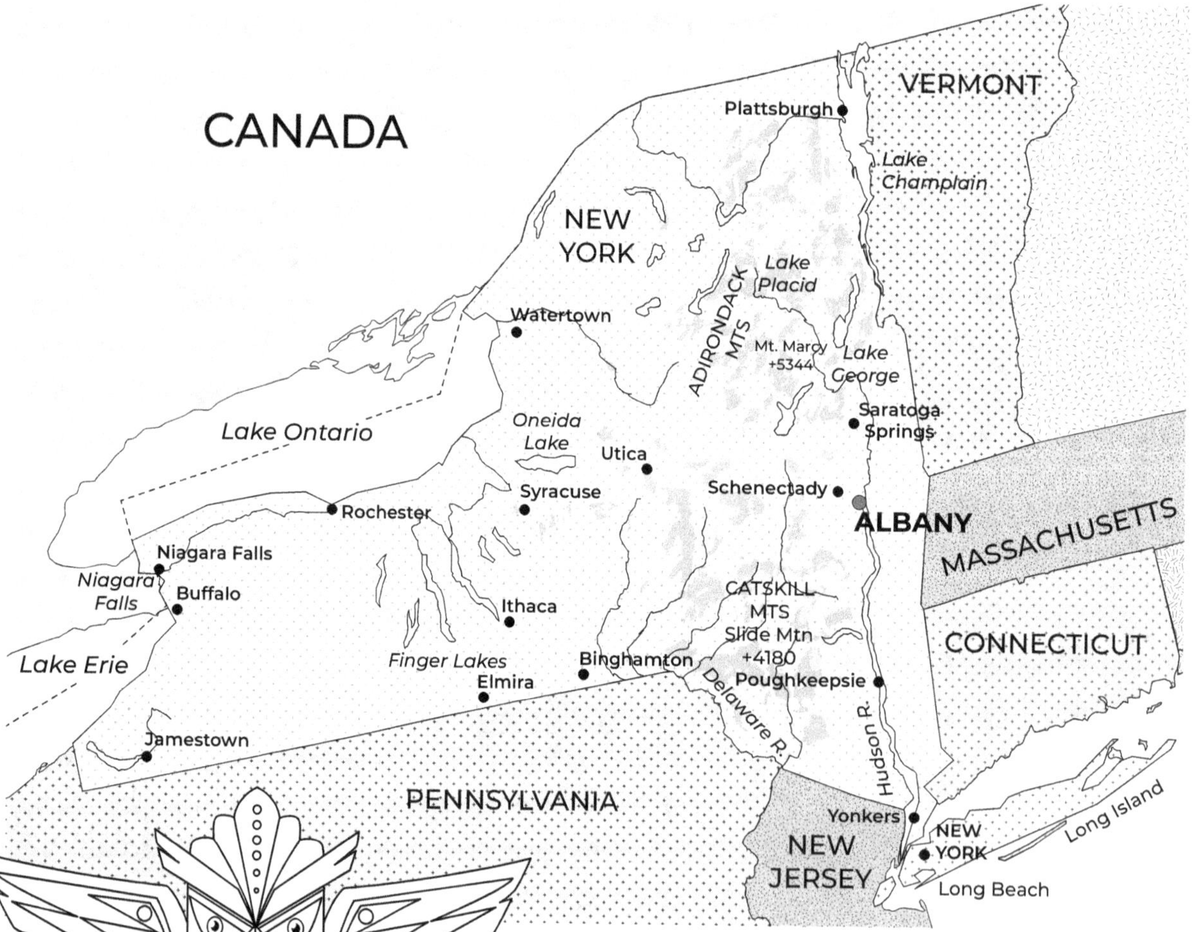

CANADA

VERMONT

Plattsburgh

Lake Champlain

NEW YORK

Lake Placid

Watertown

ADIRONDACK MTS

Mt. Marcy +5344

Lake George

Lake Ontario

Oneida Lake

Utica

Saratoga Springs

Syracuse

Schenectady

Rochester

ALBANY

MASSACHUSETTS

Niagara Falls

Niagara Falls

Buffalo

Ithaca

CATSKILL MTS

Slide Mtn +4180

CONNECTICUT

Lake Erie

Finger Lakes

Binghamton

Elmira

Delaware R.

Poughkeepsie

Hudson R.

Jamestown

PENNSYLVANIA

Yonkers

NEW JERSEY

NEW YORK

Long Island

Long Beach

" The Native American tribes who called this Northeast region of the country home depended on the **dense forests.** They would use the trees to build homes and necessary equipment or tools. They would use the tools they made to cut down more trees. By hollowing out logs, they made canoes, which gave them transportation across the lakes and rivers and increased their chances of catching fish.

The plentiful forests and bodies of water in the area created an environment full of **wildlife.** The tribes were able to hunt this wildlife, such as turkeys and moose, for food and clothing. "

1. What two Native American tribes lived in the region now known as New York State?

A. _____

B. _____

2. What is located in the Northwest region that helped the tribes survive? Select all that apply.

A. lakes

B. deserts

C. canoes

D. forests

E. clothing

3. What determined where the tribes settled down?

A. boundaries

B. laws

C. geography

D. maps

4. How was New York's diverse land beneficial for Native American groups?

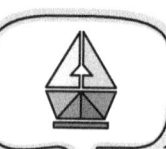
Directions: Read the text below. Then answer the questions that follow.

Yesterday you learned that the first New Yorkers were Native American tribes. Below is a map of the tribes that inhabited the area.

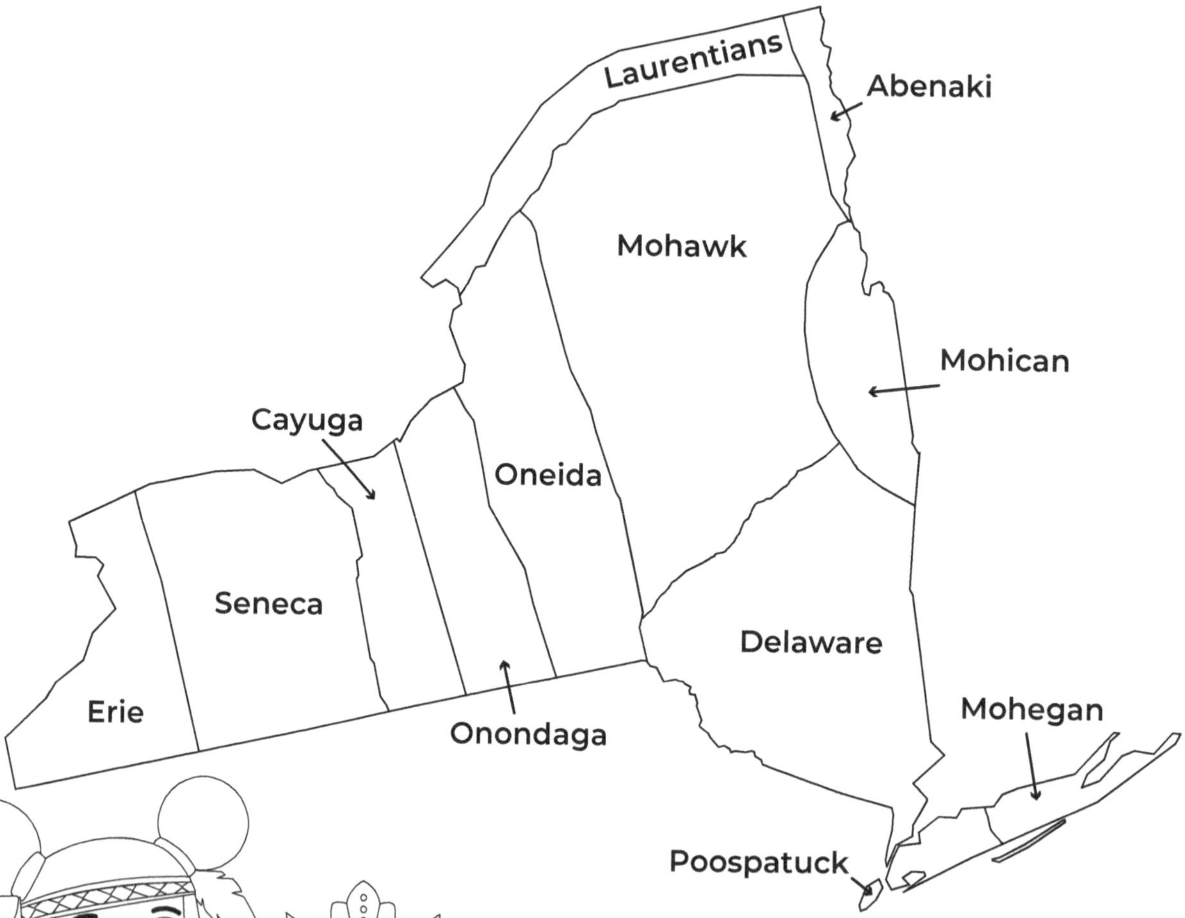

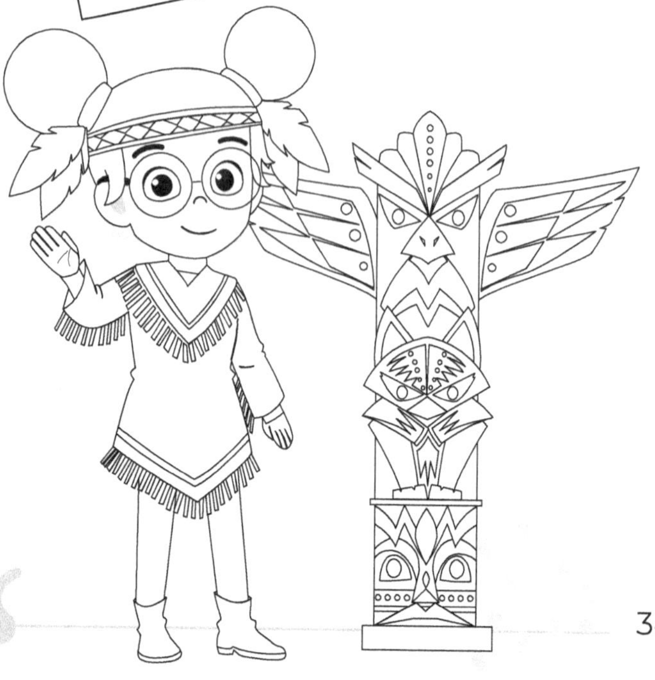

Laurentians

Abenaki

Mohawk

Mohican

Cayuga

Oneida

Seneca

Delaware

Erie

Mohegan

Onondaga

Poospatuck

34

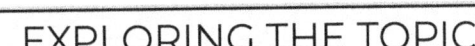

You studied the plant hardiness map in Week Two. **Plant hardiness** describes how long the growing season is in different parts of New York. **Planting season** is directly related to **climate.** The warmer colors (yellow and green) show the milder climate. The cooler colors (purple and pink) show the colder climate areas.

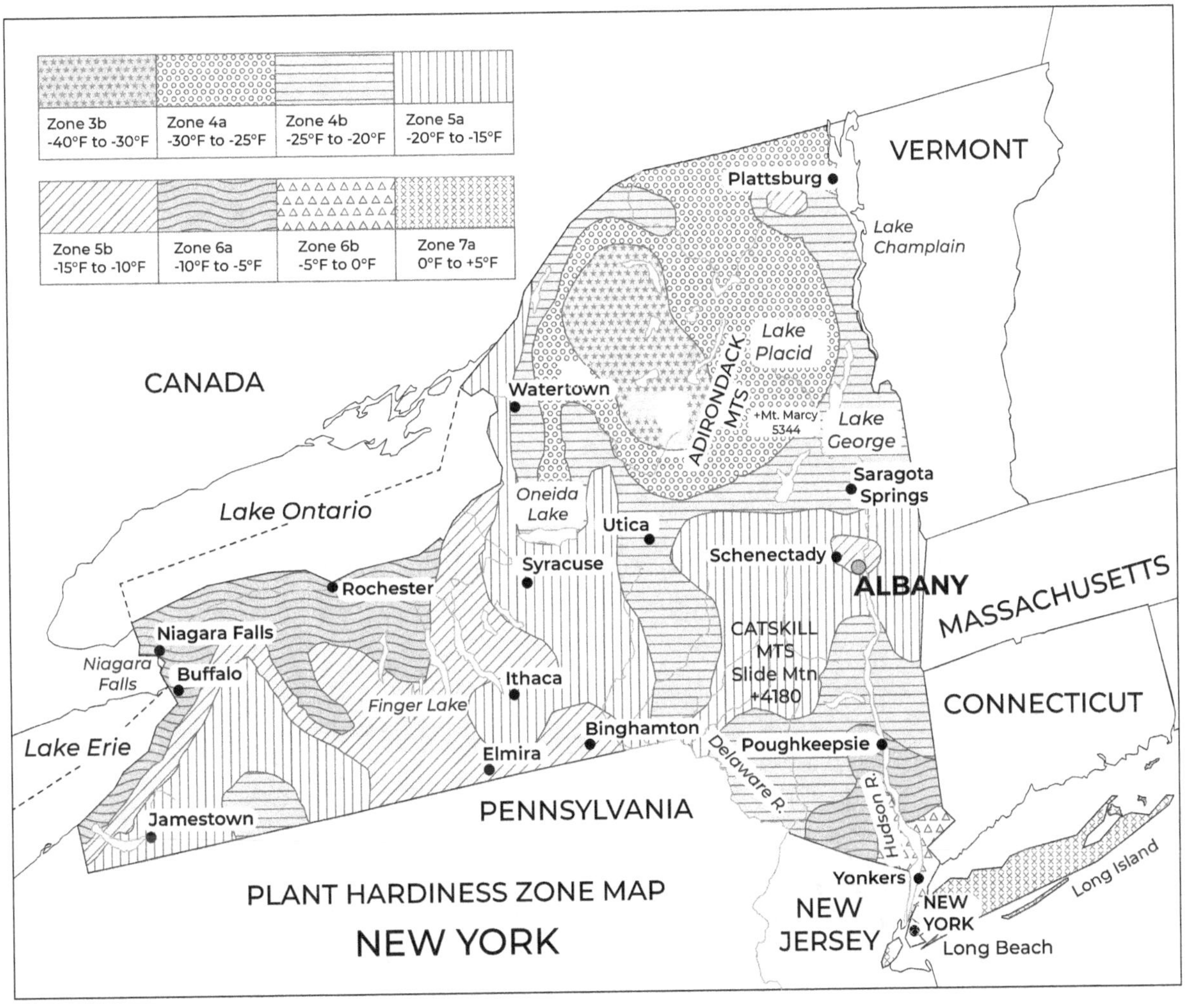

Zone 3b -40°F to -30°F	Zone 4a -30°F to -25°F	Zone 4b -25°F to -20°F	Zone 5a -20°F to -15°F
Zone 5b -15°F to -10°F	Zone 6a -10°F to -5°F	Zone 6b -5°F to 0°F	Zone 7a 0°F to +5°F

VERMONT

Plattsburg

Lake Champlain

Lake Placid

CANADA

Watertown

ADIRONDACK MTS

+Mt. Marcy 5344

Lake George

Lake Ontario

Oneida Lake

Utica

Saragota Springs

Schenectady

Rochester

Syracuse

ALBANY

MASSACHUSETTS

Niagara Falls

Niagara Falls

Buffalo

Ithaca

Finger Lake

CATSKILL MTS Slide Mtn +4180

CONNECTICUT

Lake Erie

Elmira

Binghamton

Poughkeepsie

Delaware R.

Hudson R.

Jamestown

PENNSYLVANIA

PLANT HARDINESS ZONE MAP
NEW YORK

Long Island

Yonkers

NEW JERSEY

NEW YORK

Long Beach

The climate of an area affected the Native American tribes. The milder climate areas had longer growing seasons, which meant more time to grow food. The colder climates were harder for tribes to live in. They had less access to crops, wildlife, and in some areas, the water on lakes and rivers would freeze.

Tribes throughout the region of New York all lived differently based on their environment. Their interactions became a part of their culture and made them unique from other tribes in the area.

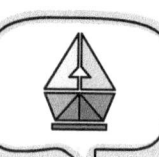
1. What Native American tribe is located Northwest of the Delaware tribe?

    A. Poospatuck

    B. Oneida

    C. Mohican

    D. Mohegan

2. Which tribe is located in the coldest climate area?

    A. Seneca

    B. Mohawk

    C. Poospatuck

    D. Cayuga

3. Which tribe has a longer growing season?

    A. Mohegan

    B. Laurentians

    C. Abenaki

    D. Mohican

4. Describe how a tribe's way of life and culture can be affected by climate.

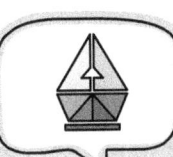
Directions: Read the text below. Then answer the questions that follow.

Iroquois
Six Nations
c. 1720

The Seneca, Cayuga, Onondaga, Oneida, and Mohawk tribes are five of the Iroquois League of Nations. These tribes lived in shelters they built called **longhouses.** These homes could hold a large number of people and had walls for protection from the weather. The tribes built longhouses close to rivers whenever possible. Having access to water was important for food preparation, fishing, hunting, and building.

These tribes were also very successful **farmers.** Among other things, they grew corn, beans, and squash. These three crops are commonly known as the "Three Sisters." Native crops, such as berries, herbs, and nuts, were gathered by tribe members. These were used for food, medicine, and dye. The Onondaga tribe also grew tobacco.

Hunting played a huge role in tribal life. The tribes in the area hunted deer and elk with bows and arrows and fished with spears and poles. These weapons were made using wood, stones, and bones. Of course, tribal members would eat the meat of the animals they killed, but they also used the bones, antlers, and furs. These materials would help them survive. Animal fur could be used to insulate walls of their longhouses and create clothing for the winter months.

In addition to using environmental resources for their basic needs, tribe members also used materials they hunted, grew, and gathered to make crafts and other items such as jewelry and baskets.

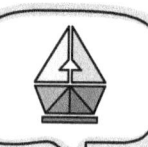
1. What type of shelter did the Iroquois tribes live in?

   A. teepee

   B. longhouse

   C. cabin

   D. brick homes

2. What crops did they grow? Select all that apply.

   A. corn

   B. tobacco

   C. melons

   D. squash

   E. potatoes

3. What are the three sisters?

   A. how many people stayed in a longhouse

   B. number of tribe members

   C. a northern tribe

   D. corn, beans and squash

4. Why were longhouses built near the river?

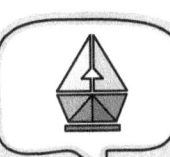
Directions: Read the text below. Then answer the questions that follow.

"

Since nature played such an important role in Native American life, tribes would often celebrate it. They would hold **ceremonies** as a sign of thanks. They depended on the environment and made sure to respect it. It was their way of giving back. Music and dancing were huge parts of these ceremonies. Tribal members would often dress up for the occasion.

Sacred masks were created and worn to represent important values and beliefs. These masks were made of carved wood and colored with the dye of plants. They were also decorated with other natural materials, such as beads, feathers, and porcupine quills.

"

1. Why did tribes celebrate nature?

....

....

2. If you were a tribe member, what would your mask look like?

3. What does your mask represent?

....

....

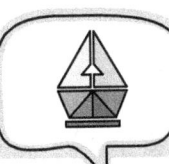
This week you learned about the Native American tribes that first inhabited the New York area. You learned that these tribes depended on the natural resources around them to survive. The physical features of an environment determined where tribes settled and how they lived. At times, tribes would adapt to or modify the land to meet their basic needs. These tribes were grateful for the gifts they received from the land.

Directions: Read the text below. Then answer the questions that follow.

Write fun facts about the Seneca tribe below by doing online research and looking at the passage on page 37. Where did the Seneca tribe live? What were their homes like? What was Seneca clothing like? .

....

....

....

....

....

....

....

....

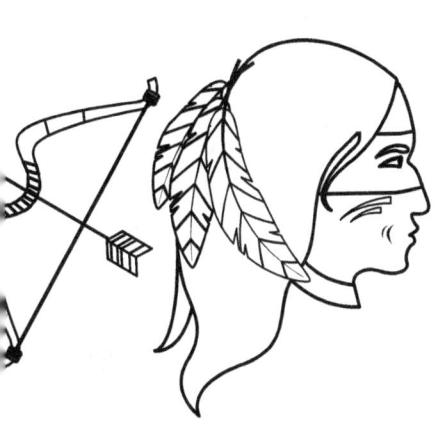

WEEK 4

Geography

Native American Tribal Life

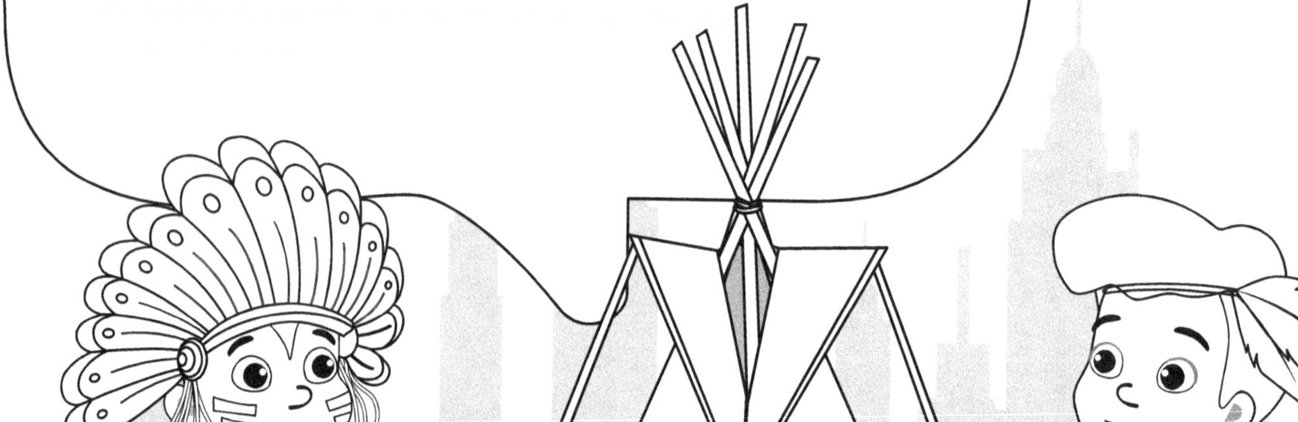

Discover Native American culture/traditions and explore how they lived as the first inhabitants of America.

ARGOPREP

Directions: Read the text below. Then answer the questions that follow.

Last week, you learned about how the Native American tribes that first lived in the New York area relied on the environment for survival. The two main groups were the **Algonquian** people and the **Iroquois**. They both built villages in the forest, hunted animals, gathered plants, and farmed crops. They did not, however, speak the same language.

Several Iroquois tribes formed a **confederacy,** also known as the Five Nations. The confederacy brought tribes together and kept the peace. The tribes were no longer fighting with each other. The group would meet regularly for **Grand Council** meetings. Each tribe would send a chief to these meetings to represent them. Grand Council discussed topics such as peace, trade, land use, and war with the Algonquians.

The five Iroquois tribes that were a part of the Five Nations were the Seneca, Cayuga, Onondaga, Oneida, and Mohawk. Their dedication to living peacefully and working together made them one of the most powerful Native American confederacies in North America.

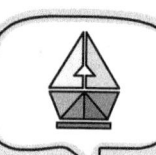
1. What is the major difference between the Algonquain and Iroquois tribes?

    A. villages

    B. chiefs

    C. farming

    D. language

2. What was the main purpose of the Five Nations?

    A. fighting

    B. peace

    C. leadership

    D. farming

3. Which of these tribes was NOT part of the Five Nations?

    A. Mohawk

    B. Onondaga

    C. Algonquain

    D. Cayuga

4. Was the formation of the Five Nations successful? Why or why not?

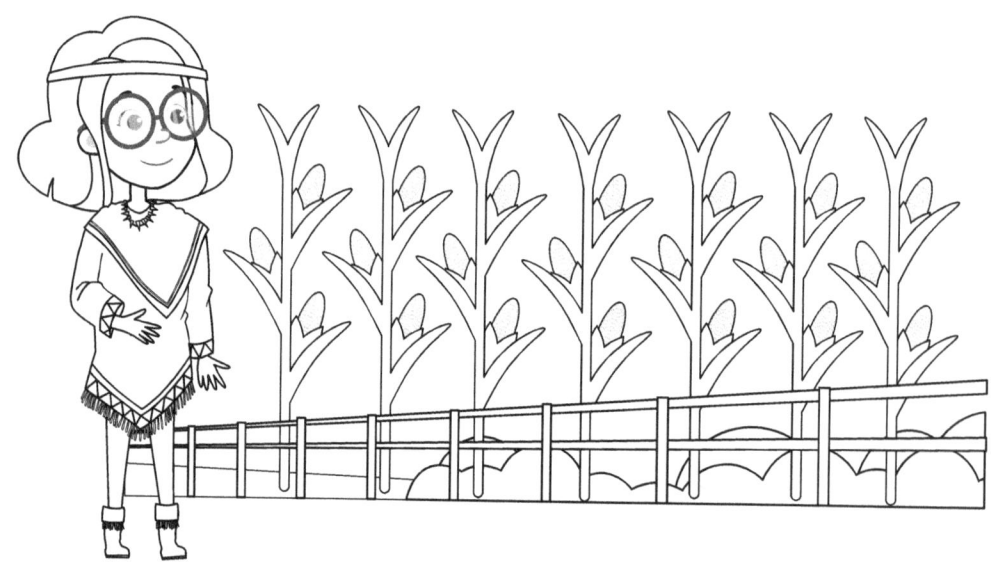

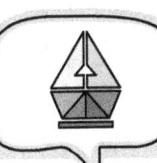
Directions: Read the text below. Then answer the questions that follow.

The **Iroquois** called themselves "People of the Longhouse" or Haudenosaunee. **Longhouses** were really long dwellings. They could be from 40 to 100 feet long. Members of an entire **clan** lived together in a longhouse. A clan was a large extended family who all shared a common ancestor.

The leaders of these clans were the women. They were called **clan mothers.** They had a lot of power in Iroquois villages. They were in charge of the longhouses and made decisions about how to use the village's farmland. They were the farmers and the gatherers. The women were also in charge of choosing **sachems,** or chiefs.

While the women made important decisions about how the village would run, the men handled hunting, trading, and war. The chiefs who were appointed would attend Grand Council to help make government decisions. They discussed the territory and where village sites should be located.

Native American children played a very important role in the tribe. Girls would gather plants with their mothers, help make meals, and weave. Boys would go fishing and hunting with their fathers. They learned about trading and war. Children had many responsibilities to keep the tribe running smoothly, but they also took the time to have fun.

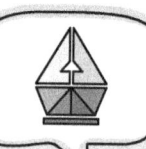
1. What is a clan?

   A. an ancestor

   B. large family

   C. a group of chiefs

   D. a type of longhouse

2. Who held the most power in the clan?

   A. chiefs

   B. women

   C. men

   D. children

3. Who was in charge of trading?

   A. men of the tribe

   B. clan mothers

   C. children

   D. sachems

4. The children in the tribe had no responsibilities.

   A. True

   B. False

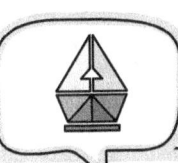
Directions: Read the text below. Then answer the questions that follow.

Yesterday you learned that the women were in charge of the clans and village. Societies that have women as leaders are known as **matriarchal societies.** The mothers were the head of the family and the clan. They made important decisions and were highly valued. They named the chiefs who would go to council to keep the peace and make goverment decisions about their land.

However, not all tribes that lived in the New York area were run by women. One example is the **Mohican** nation that lived along the east bank of the Hudson River. They were divided into three clans: the bear, the wolf, and the turtle. This nation was not part of the League of Nations and was often at war with the Mohawk. Women were not leaders in their tribe. Each village had its own chief that they inherited through their mother's side of the family.

Even though the society structure of the Mohican tribe was different from most other tribes in New York, the responsibilities were primarily the same. Women in the Mohican tribe farmed and gathered resources from the environment such as fruit and nuts. The men hunted in the woods and handled all trading. The copper found in their area was used to trade with other tribal nations.

1. What is the definition of a matriarchal society?

   A. peaceful decision making

   B. women are in charge

   C. trading with other tribes

   D. having clans

2. All Native American tribes in the New York area had a matriarchal society.

   A. True

   B. False

3. Compare and contrast the Mohican tribe with the tribes in the League of Nations.

Directions: Read the text below. Then answer the questions that follow.

Native Americans lived in North America long before the European settlers arrived. They learned how to live off of the land, run successful villages, and get along with one another. There are many ways that their inventions, accomplishments, and way of life influenced our lives.

The **Iroquois League** was an advanced system of negotiating. American government today still uses this basic power distribution. There was one central authority, and then the power branched out to individual village chiefs. In our government today, there is a main federal government (president) that branches out to state (governers) and local governments (mayors).

Native Americans learned to farm the foods that we still eat today such as corn, peanuts, and squash. They also learned valuable information about the power of plants in curing diseases. Some of the medicines we have on the market today rely on plants.

We can also thank Native Americans for their artistic handwork. Many of their techniques, such as weaving, beading, and pottery, are still used today. Tribal ceremonies with special clothing or costumes, music, food, and dancing are another tradition that we have taken and made our own. Most people today have large get-togethers or parties to celebrate the lives of friends and family members.

1. Describe at least two ways that Native American culture has influenced your life.

....

....

....

2. What can we learn from Native Americans about environmental resources?

....

....

....

This week you learned about Native American tribal life. Most tribes had an advanced system of responsibility and cooperation. Each tribal member knew their role in the tribe, and everyone played their part. You learned about how the Iroquois League was arranged and why. Also, you read about the jobs of women, men, and children, and their expectations within the tribe.

Directions: Read the text below. Then answer the questions that follow.

Choose from one of the following tribal roles: Clan mother, Chief, Child. Write a journal entry that describes what your day is like in that role. Use the information you learned this week to add detail to your entry.

Geography
European Explorers

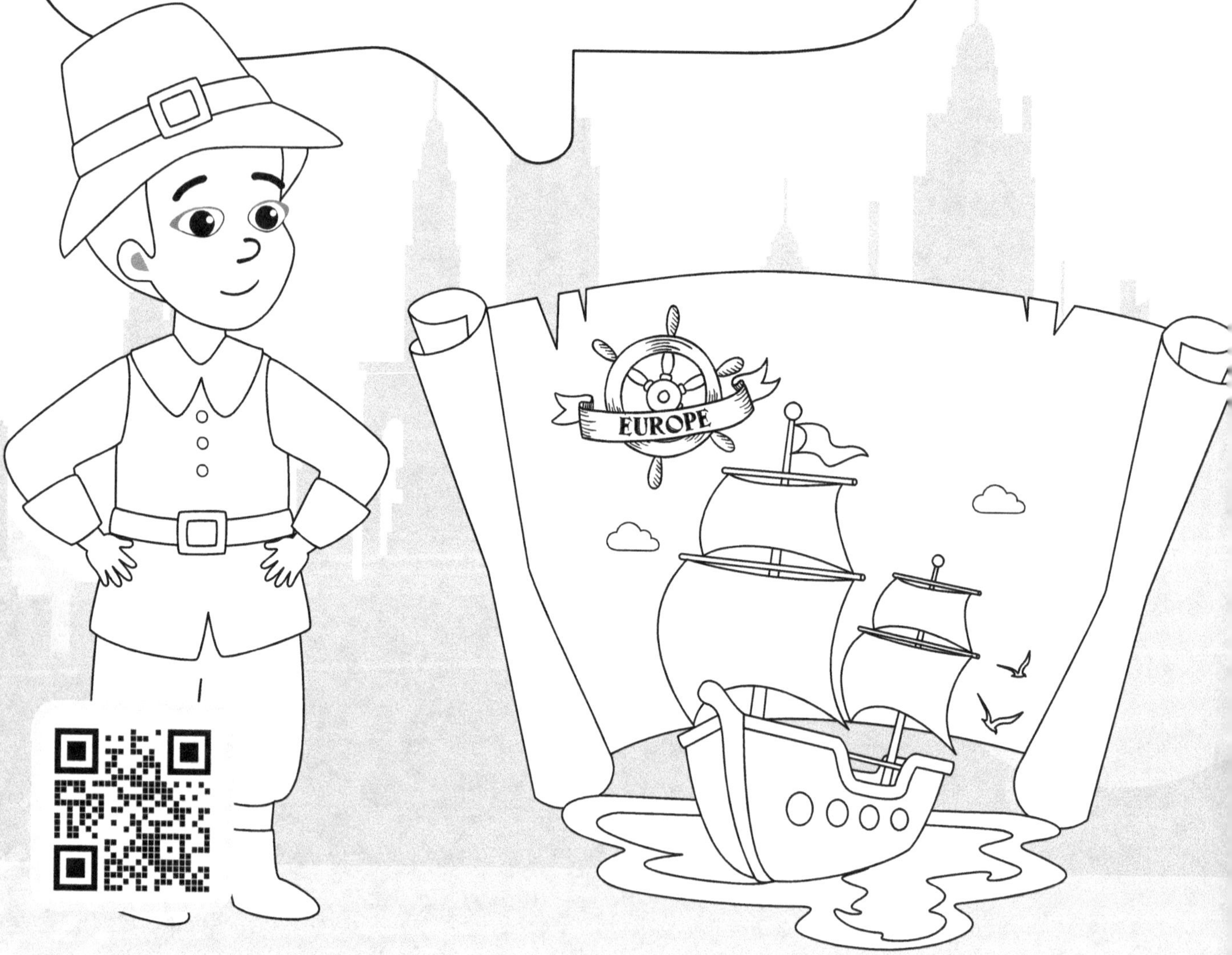

Learn about European explorers and their journey to North America.

ARGOPREP

Directions: Read the text below. Then answer the questions that follow.

The continents of Europe and Asia lie across the Atlantic Ocean from North America. New York is located in North America. You can see them on the map below.

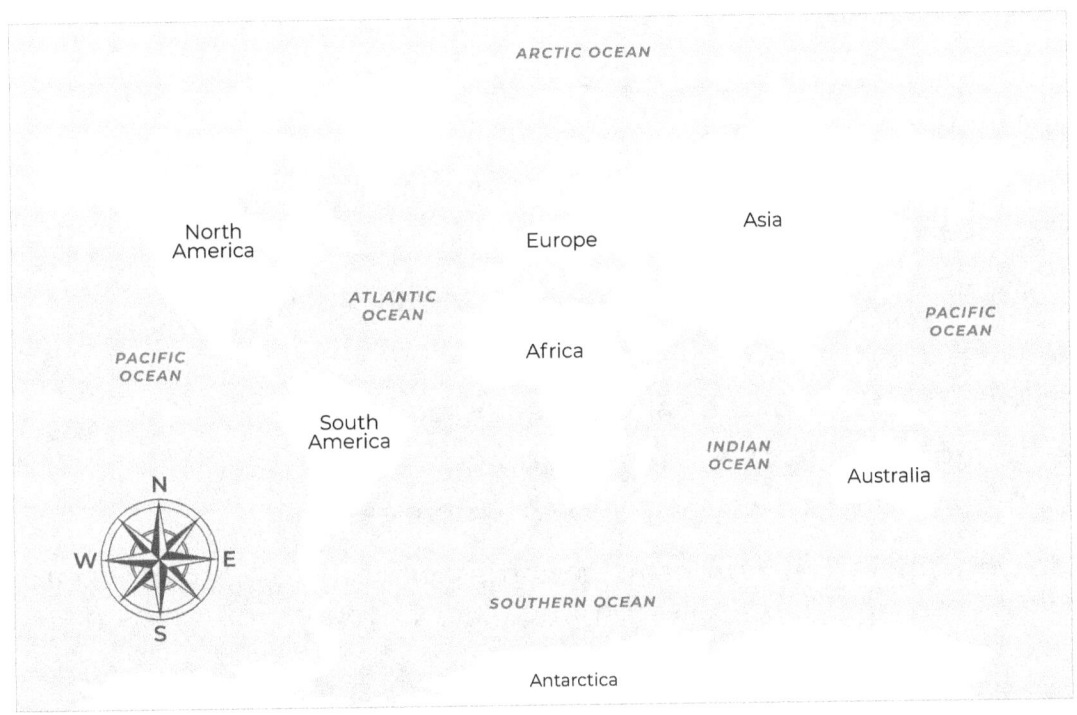

Explorers from many European countries wanted to get to **Asia.** Asia had goods that countries in Europe wanted such as silk and spices. Trade between Europe and Asia was an important and growing business. However, getting to Asia from Europe heading east was difficult. The trip was long and required explorers to travel through mountain ranges, making it dangerous. On one expedition, explorers heading west ran into **North America** – a continent they didn't even know existed!

Kings across Europe heard the news of this new land and started to hire explorers to sail west. At the time, they were most interested in North America because they thought it was a new way to get to Asia. They wanted the explorers they hired to find the best way through the new land. This route became known as the **Northwest Passage.**

Rulers throughout Europe wanted their country to be the first to find the Northwest Passage that would lead them to Asia. Many of the voyages that explorers took concluded near the land that is known today as New York.

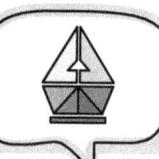
1. What continent were European explorers looking for?

   A. North America

   B. Europe

   C. Asia

   D. Northwest Passage

2. Why did the explorers go west to get to Asia?

   A. The traders were on the other side of Asia.

   B. Travel to Asia from the east was very difficult.

   C. The kings wanted the explorers to find new land.

   D. Asia is located west of Europe.

3. Why were the kings excited about the Northwest Passage?

   A. They wanted to take over the land.

   B. They knew they could trade along the passage.

   C. They thought it was better than finding Asia.

   D. They thought it was a way to get to Asia more easily.

4. Why do you think that European countries wanted to be the first to find the Northwest Passage? Use details from the text to support your thinking.

Directions: Read the text below. Then answer the questions that follow.

There were several explorers who made important discoveries in the New York State area. They all shared the desire to find the **Northwest Passage.**

In 1497, **John Cabot** made the trip west from the country of England. He reached the land of Canada, thinking he had made it to Asia.

Giovanni da Verrazzano, an explorer from Italy, became the first European to see New York Bay in 1524. He immediately knew when he reached the shore that he was not in Asia.

In 1534, the explorer **Cartier** sailed to France. He traveled up the St. Lawrence River trying to find the Northwest Passage.

Cartier was followed by **Samuel de Champlain** in 1608. Champlain, also sailing for France, reached what is now called Lake Champlain in 1609.

Henry Hudson was an explorer for the Netherlands (Dutch). In 1609, he traveled up the Hudson River to what is now known as Albany.

Even though all these European countries were determined to find the Northwest Passage, they never did. Instead, these explorers discovered a new land, the land of the Native American tribes. The explorers encountered and interacted with the Native American people, which changed the way of life for both the explorers and the first New Yorkers.

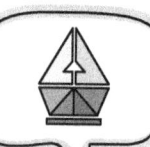

1. What do all the explorers from Europe have in common?

   A. They all sailed from the same country.

   B. They made the same discoveries.

   C. They all were looking for the Northwest Passage.

   D. They found an easier route to Asia.

2. Which explorer did not make it to the New York area?

   A. Cartier

   B. Hudson

   C. Verrazzano

   D. Cabot

3. Draw lines on the map to mark the routes that each of the following explorers took: Cabot, Verrazzano, Champlain, and Hudson.

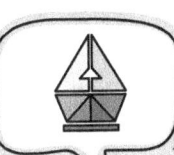
Directions: Read the text below. Then answer the questions that follow.

Earlier this week, you learned that several European countries sent explorers west in search of a safe route to Asia. However, they made new discoveries in North America, a land that they did not know of before.

In 1523, **Giovanni da Verrazzano** was commissioned by the King of France to find a passageway to Asia through the new land. The country of France was in competition with other European countries to find the easiest and quickest way to Asia. Verranzzano set sail in 1524 from Portugal and landed off the coast of North Carolina. Over several days, he headed north up the coastline, eventually sailing into New York Bay. In his journal entries that he wrote during his travels, Verrazzano noted the beautiful land was full of trees and crops were growing. He knew this place was a land of opportunity.

Samuel de Champlain, a professional mapmaker from France, first landed in North America in 1603. He interacted with the Native Americans more than any other European had at that time in history. He was interested in trading. However, Champlain arrived at a time when many of the Indian nations were at war with one another. Without peace in the land, there could be no trade, so Champlain was determined to help bring peace. He was able to do so by gaining each nation's trust. The only tribe that did not cooperate was the Mohawks. They were very skilled warriors. Champlain knew the only way to get around them was to fight. He and the Indian nation of Canada banned together to defeat the Mohawk tribe.

Henry Hudson was born in England to a family that owned a trading company. Since everyone else was heading west, Hudson decided to sail north. However, that journey proved to be as dangerous as heading east to Asia. In 1609, he sailed again, funded by the Netherlands, heading west. He landed in Maine and traveled south until he reached the Hudson River. He claimed the land he found for the Netherlands. This land today is known as New York City. On another expedition in 1610, Hudson located the Hudson Bay. His crew left him there, and he was never seen again.

1. What European country did each of the following explorers sail for?

   A. Verrazzano

   B. Champlain

   C. Hudson

2. What did Verrazzano notice about the land of North America?

3. Explain Champlain's interactions with the Native American tribes during his exploration.

4. What is significant about Henry Hudson's discoveries while in North America?

Directions: Read the text below. Then answer the questions that follow.

You have learned all about the European explorers who were significant to discovering what is now the state of New York. As you know, they were all in search of Asia. They needed a quick and easy way to access the many riches, such as spices, that existed throughout the continent. Having access to these resources would lead to better trade deals. Therefore, European countries were willing to pay for explorers to take long and expensive journeys to find their way.

Below is a **climate map.** You will notice that Europe and Asia are labeled, as well as the huge mountain range that lies between them. Without those mountains, the Europeans would have easily made the trip to other Asian countries.

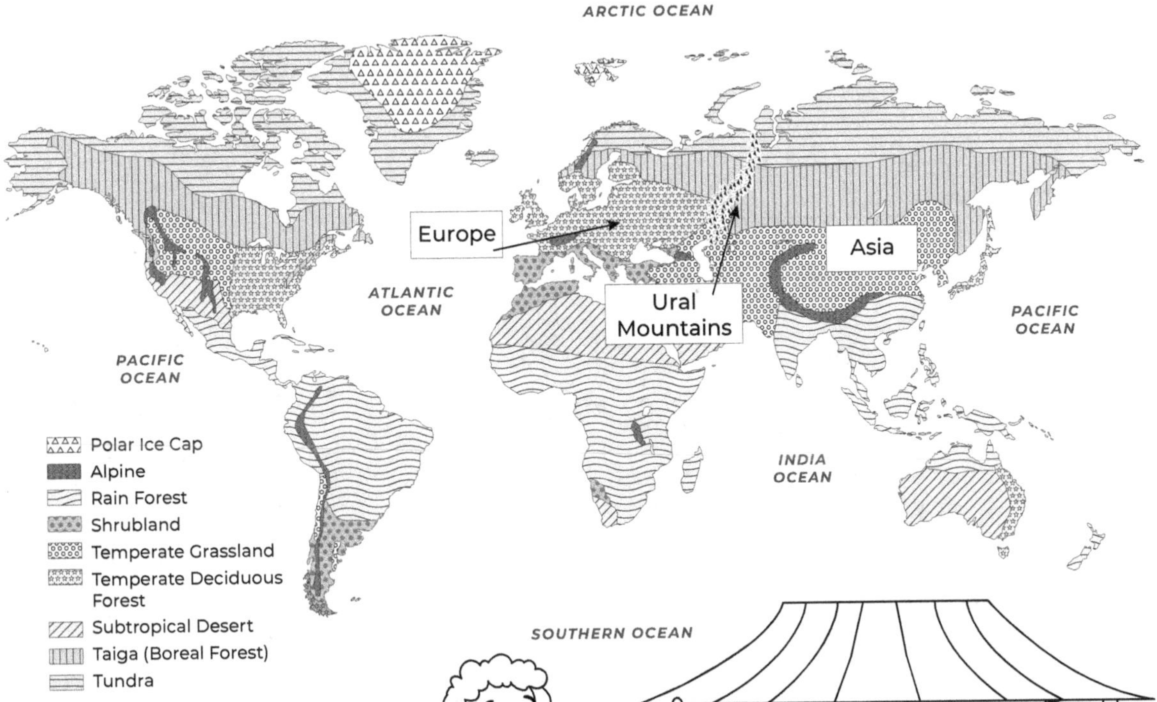

ARCTIC OCEAN

Europe

Asia

ATLANTIC OCEAN

Ural Mountains

PACIFIC OCEAN

PACIFIC OCEAN

INDIA OCEAN

- Polar Ice Cap
- Alpine
- Rain Forest
- Shrubland
- Temperate Grassland
- Temperate Deciduous Forest
- Subtropical Desert
- Taiga (Boreal Forest)
- Tundra

SOUTHERN OCEAN

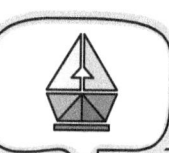
1. What routes were possible for the explorers to take by water to get from Europe to Asia? Use your pencil to draw possible routes on the map.

2. You will notice on the climate map that the top countries have polar climates. What problems would this have caused for explorers?

....

....

....

....

3. If you were an explorer, what route would you have tried to get to Asia quickly and safely?

....

....

....

....

This week you learned about European explorers who discovered New York waterways in their quests to find Asia. These men included Verrazzano, Champlain, and Hudson. They were the first to encounter the Native American people of the Algonquian and Iroquois nations. The European discovery of this new land led to the development of early settlements and trade posts, as well as the struggle over land ownership.

Directions: Read the text below. Then answer the questions that follow.

1. Complete the cause and effect chart using the information you learned this week.

Cause (Why Something Happened)	Effect (What Happened)
The mountain range that lies between Europe and Asia was difficult to cross.	
	The explorers discovered North America.
	Champlain made allies with many Indian nations.
Henry Hudson claimed the land he found for the Netherlands.	

2. Now that the Europeans know of this new land in North America, what do you predict happened next? Why?

....

....

....

....

History

European Settlement

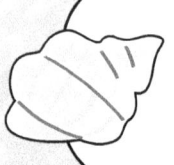

WEEK 6

Learn about European settlers and how they started a new life in North America.

ARGOPREP

Directions: Read the text below. Then answer the questions that follow.

Last week you learned about the European explorers who arrived in North America. Their arrival started a wave of settlers moving into the new land. After failing at finding a passageway to Asia, Europeans were anxious to farm the land and begin trading.

Based on Henry Hudson's exploration in 1609, the Dutch claimed the land along the Hudson River and on Manhattan Island. The **Dutch West India Company** was the first European settlement in New York. It was established in 1624 as a fur trading post called **Fort Orange.** The Dutch called their land **New Netherland,** named after their home country.

In 1626, the Dutch established another settlement. It was called **New Amsterdam,** and it was located on Manhattan Island. This land had long belonged to the Algonquian tribe called **Lenni Lanape.**

Close to five thousand colonists were living in the New York area by 1660. Of these colonists, two-thirds were from the Netherlands (Dutch). The rest were from the countries of France, England, Sweden, Finland, and the continent of Africa. These settlers were in a whole new land, and they were excited about the opportunities before them.

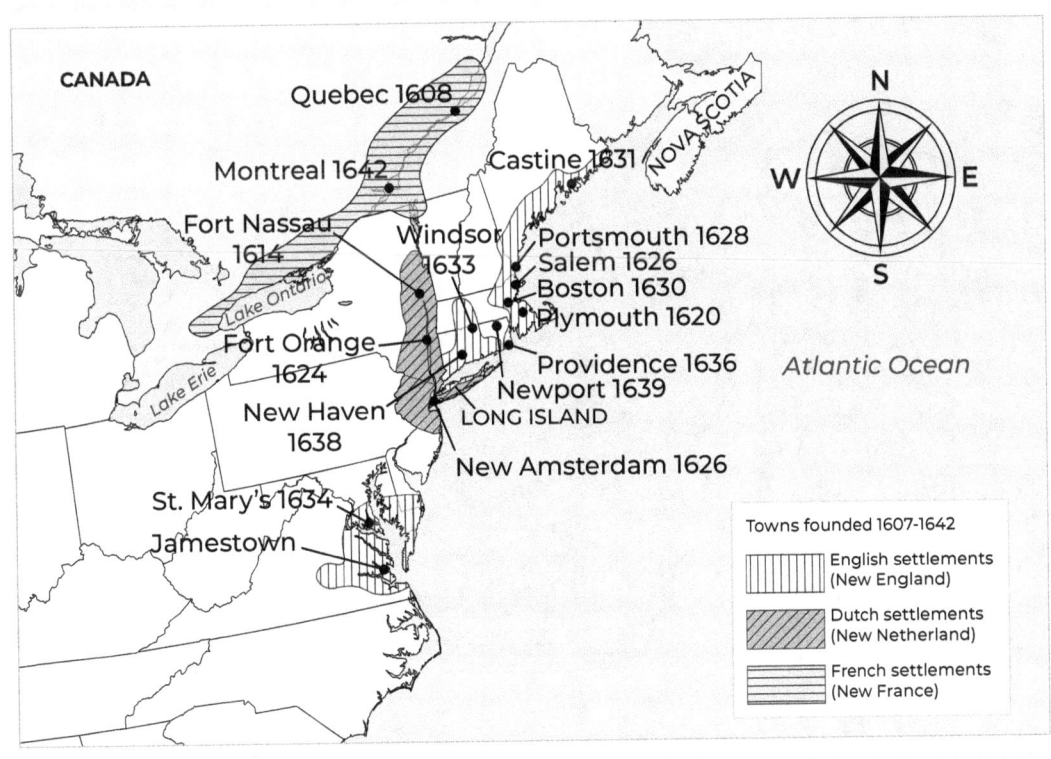

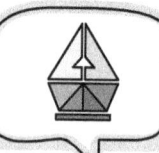
1. What year did the Dutch West India Company establish the first European settlement?

    A. 1609
    B. 1624
    C. 1626
    D. 1660

2. What was the Dutch fur trading post called?

    A. Manhattan Island
    B. Lenni Lanape
    C. Fort Orange
    D. New Netherland

3. Which European country had the largest amount of settlers in the New York area?

    A. France
    B. Sweden
    C. England
    D. Netherlands (Dutch)

4. The Lenni Lanape tribe was part of the Iroquois Nation.

    A. True
    B. False

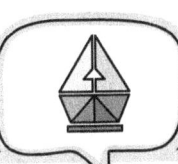
Directions: Read the text below. Then answer the questions that follow.

Native Americans had been living in what is now New York for years. European explorers came in search of a place where they could trade. The land of North America seemed to provide what they were looking for. European countries began to quickly claim the land for themselves before another country did. They began to send colonists to settle there.

The purpose of the **Dutch West India Company** trade post was to interact and exchange goods with the Native Americans. The Europeans wanted to trade fur and timber. Their company became the center of the Dutch fur trade. The Dutch claimed part of New York, New Jersey, Connecticut, and Delaware.

As you learned yesterday, the **Lenni Lenape** called the island of Manhattan home. When the settlers arrived, they built homes on the island and changed its name to "New Amsterdam." In 1626, **Peter Minuit** traveled to New Amsterdam to lead the new settlement. He convinced the Lenni Lenape to sell their land to him. He bought the land with some tools and other items such as pots. The idea of "owning land" was foreign to the Native Americans. They did not believe that man could own land. When they made the deal with Minuit, they thought they were agreeing to share the land's resources with him and his fellow Dutch.

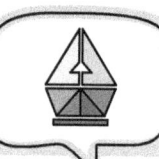
1. What goods were the Dutch trading with the Native Americans? Select all that apply.

   A. corn

   B. fur

   C. arrows

   D. timber

   E. longhouses

2. Who was Peter Minuit?

   A. Lenni Lenape chief

   B. New Amsterdam leader

   C. Dutch explorer

   D. fur trapper

3. Explain how the Dutch got control of New Amsterdam (Manhattan).

Directions: Read the text below. Then answer the questions that follow.

The fur trade was a very profitable business in the colony of New Netherland and its capital city, New Amsterdam. It kept bringing more and more settlers to the New York area. The **Dutch West India Company** encouraged people from many different cultures to settle there. There were several European countries and religions represented in the settlement.

Native Americans brought beaver and other animal skins to the **Fort Orange** trading post. They bartered for goods that they did not have access to such as metal tools, knives, axes, and cloth. The **Hudson River** was then used as a port to ship off the furs they acquired. Beaver furs were very popular and hard to find in Europe. The Dutch were able to sell the furs in many European countries.

The Dutch West India company wanted more settlers to come to their land. More settlers would mean more money. The newcomers could farm and make the goods to trade with the Native Americans for furs. To attract more settlers, the Dutch company offered to give large pieces of land to those that could send at least fifty more people to the new land. Those who agreed to the deal were known as **patroons.** A patroon would own the land he was given, and the settlers he paid to bring to the colony would work on his land. They would pay rent by giving up some of the crops they grew.

When the first European settlers came to New York, the lives of Native Americans began to change drastically. Of course, the settlers began to invade and take over the Native American land. The Europeans introduced different **textiles** to the natives, such as wool and cotton. As a result, Native Americans began to use these materials to make their clothing and blankets. The Europeans also introduced Native Americans to metal fish hooks, as opposed to the bone hooks they had been using. This changed their approach to fishing. Unfortunately, the settlers also brought **diseases** with them, such as measles, which were deadly to the native tribes.

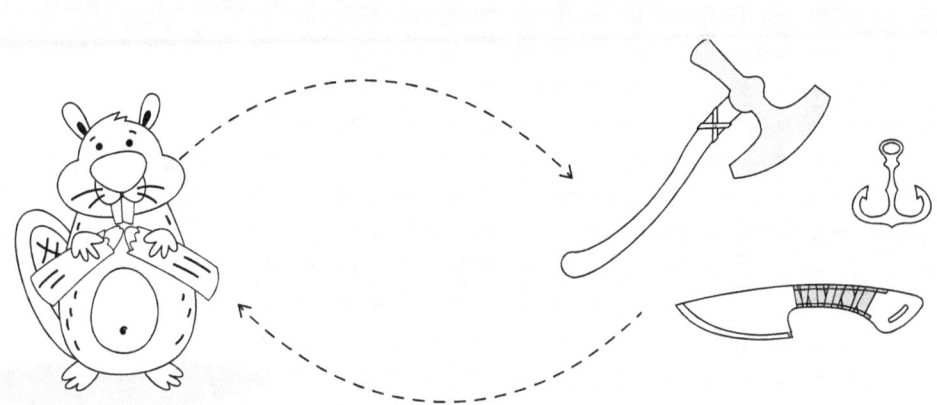

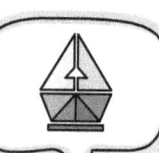
1. Explain how the Dutch West India Company made money by trading with the Native Americans.

2. Why did the Native Americans want to trade their beaver furs?

3. In what ways did the European arrival negatively impact the Native Americans?

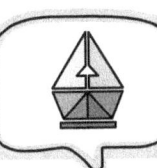
Directions: Read the text below. Then answer the questions that follow.

"

The **Dutch** started the colony of New Netherland in the hopes of a successful fur trade business with the **Algonquin Indians.** They made money for quite a while. However, the Dutch West India Company started to lose money because too many animals were being hunted. The Native Americans were so eager to get their hands on new tools and equipment that they were hunting beavers at an alarming rate. Also, there was fighting between the colonists and the Lenni Lenape. The Native Americans felt tricked into giving up their rights to land they felt everyone should have access to. There was distrust between settlers and the native people, which was causing the colony to unravel. The Dutch West India Company decided that a governor was necessary to improve the colony.

Peter Stuyvesant, also known as "Stubborn Pete," was not a well-liked governor. He had a bad temper, and he tried to remove certain groups from the colony. For example, he wanted to make the Jewish colonists leave the colony. The Dutch West India Company would not allow him to remove any groups of people. Although he had his flaws, Stuyvesant did accomplish some good for the colony. He paved the streets and fixed buildings. He made peace with the Native Americans, on behalf of the colonists, and made the colony a safer place for all. The Dutch began to see some hope for the future.

"

1. Why was the fur trade struggling to succeed?

....

....

2. Why were the Lenni Lenape and colonists fighting?

....

....

3. The Dutch West India Company wanted more settlers to come. What do you think Stuyvesant's reasoning was for trying to remove groups from the colony?

....

....

Directions: Read the text below. Then answer the questions that follow.

This week you learned all about European settlements in the New York area colonies. The colonists used their resources to trade with the Native Americans for valuable furs. They would then send the furs back to their home country. This was a very profitable business. You also learned how the Native Americans benefited from this European influence.

However, the Dutch were not the only Europeans who had discovered North America. The **English** also had laid claims in North America. In fact, they explored and claimed the land where the Dutch settled before the Dutch actually made their claim. In 1664, the English sent in warships to take back their land from the Dutch. The Dutch did not put up a fight because they were outnumbered. They immediately surrendered. The King of England gifted the land to his brother, **The Duke of York.** Therefore, the English changed the name of the town from New Amsterdam to **New York.** They also changed the name of Fort Orange to **Albany.** New York was governed as a royal colony, which means the colonists were able to elect representatives for their government.

New York was greatly influenced by the Dutch. Its economy continued to grow thanks to the fur trade they developed. The Dutch were very accepting of colonists with different backgrounds and religious beliefs. These values remained even after the English took over.

Explain both the positive and negative effects of European settlement in New York. Use the information you learned this week to answer.

....

....

....

....

....

....

....

WEEK 7

History
Colonial Times

Learn about the economy, labor, and slave trades during colonial times.

ARGOPREP

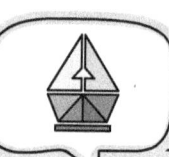
Directions: Read the text below. Then answer the questions that follow.

When Peter Stuyvesant handed over control of the New Netherland colony to the English, Dutch control came to an end. They had influenced the area for over 40 years. The English decided to divide the colony into two parts. The smaller area became **New Jersey,** and the the larger area was called **New York.** The town of New Amsterdam was renamed **New York City.**

Even though they no longer controlled the land, many of the Dutch colonists stayed. They were allowed to keep their jobs and ownership of their land. However, they had to swear their loyalty to the King of England. The Dutch and the English people got along well. They even shared a church together.

Albany and New York City remained **major trading centers** for the colony. New Yorkers traded goods, such as lumber, with England and their other colonies. **Ship building** also became an important part of the economy. This new venture led to new jobs, which meant that more colonists were needed. They needed people to make rope, weave linen, and make sails. This business made fur trade less important. **Whaling** for blubber also became a way for the colonists to feed their growing economy.

Since the colony was doing so well, people came from all over world to settle in New York. They came for a variety of different reasons. Some were hoping to find land. Many people came for the job opportunities. There were also a few that came for religious freedom.

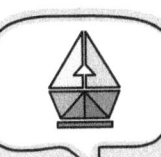
1. How did the New Netherland colony change when the English took over? Select all that apply.

   A. They moved to a new location.

   B. They split the colony into two parts.

   C. They renamed the colony "New York."

   D. Most of the Dutch left the colony.

   E. The economy began to suffer.

2. If you were a Dutch colonist who wanted to stay in the New York colony, what would you have to do?

   A. You had to buy your land from the English.

   B. You needed to find a different job.

   C. You had move away from the English colonists.

   D. You had to pledge your loyalty to the King.

3. What new business did the New York Colony start?

   A. weaving

   B. shipbuilding

   C. farming

   D. fur trading

4. What were three of the reasons that people came to settle in New York?

   A. _____

   B. _____

   C. _____

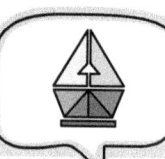
Directions: Read the text below. Then answer the questions that follow.

By 1733, England had **13 colonies** along the eastern shore of North America. More and more colonists came from countries such as Germany, France, Scotland, and continents such as Africa. When colonists came, they brought their traditions and beliefs with them to the colonies. As the number of colonists grew, they took over more and more of the Native American lands. Naturally, this led to more disagreements between the colonists and Native Americans.

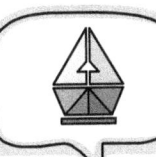
"New York played an early role in the slave trade. Both the Dutch and the English used enslaved people for labor. When England first took over the colonies, there were several hundred **Africans** living in the area. Some of these Africans were free and even owned land, but most were **slaves.** Over the next hundred years, the African population in the colonies rose to about 20,000. This was mostly due to the slave trade.

By the end of the 1700s, New York had the largest African population of any northern English state. These enslaved people were shipped against their will to the port in New York monthly and auctioned off to the highest bidder. They performed manual labor and were not paid for their work. Slaves performed numerous jobs for the colonists. They worked on farms, in homes, and as artisans, such as blacksmiths, carpenters, and weavers."

1. How many English colonies were there in the early 1700s?

   A. 2
   B. hundreds
   C. 13
   D. 20,000

2. What was the effect of so many colonists settling in the area?

   A. They could not find jobs.
   B. More Native American lands were taken.
   C. They realized they would rather go back home.
   D. They took control of the English colonies.

3. Explain how New York was involved in the early slave trade.

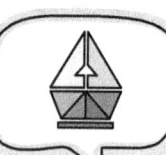
Directions: Read the text below. Then answer the questions that follow.

Yesterday you learned that New York was involved in the **early slave trade.** The colonists had access to a ton of land to farm, trade, and craft. Very early on, they used enslaved Africans for free labor. Although both the Dutch and the English had slaves, African Americans had different experiences under the two European groups.

When the **Dutch** ruled the land, from 1621 to 1664, they used slaves to construct roads and buildings, saw trees, and prepare the land for farming. The enslaved learned the Dutch language and took on many other elements of their culture. They were granted partial freedom in the 1640s. They were allowed to farm their own land and sell their crops, but they were required to pay taxes and work for the colony when asked. They could only live in the same community as other former slaves.

Under **British** rule, from 1664 to 1776, slavery greatly expanded. The British were far harsher regarding their enslaved people than the Dutch were. The British had rules for when slaves could come and go and who they could speak to. Slaves lived in homes with their white owners and followed their owner's demands. Some worked in the fields or the homes, while others were taught a specific skill, like carpentry. Most slaves were freed by 1827.

Throughout the colonial period, some slaves escaped to Native American lands. Many Native Americans welcomed and helped them. Escaping was very risky. If they were caught, the enslaved were usually harshly punished.

Compare and contrast the experiences enslaved Africans had under the two periods.

Dutch Period   **Both**   **English Period**

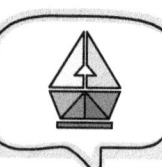
Directions: Read the text below. Then answer the questions that follow.

You have learned how the enslaved people in the colony had different experiences under Dutch and English rule. However, the enslaved were not the only ones who felt a change when the Dutch lost control of the land. The **structure of government** in the colony changed. People from the colonies elected colonists to an assembly. The only colonists who could vote were white men. However, they could not vote for their governor. That was decided by the British leaders.

It was against the law to speak out against the government. In 1733, **Peter Zenger** started a newspaper called The New-York Weekly Journal. In his paper, he criticized the actions of William Cosby, the governor at the time. He wrote that he was greedy and abusing his power. These statements were true. Zenger was arrested when he would not give up the name of who wrote the articles. Zenger and his lawyer believed that as long as what was printed was true, anyone should be allowed to speak about the government. His case went to trial, and he was found not guilty. This case later led to the establishment of a free press in America. **Freedom of the press** and **freedom of speech** are important parts of America's constitution.

Children in the colony were also affected by the change in leadership. In New Amsterdam, children went to school year round. In the English colony, children went to school for about 3 months a year. Boys typically attended school for about three years and girls went for an even shorter time. Classes that had once been taught in Dutch were changed to English. Schooling was no longer free for the public, and families had to pay for their child to attend. Many children focused on learning a skill or trade that they could use in the colony.

1. Who elected the governor of a colony?

   A. colonists

   B. white men

   C. British leaders

   D. Dutch settlers

2. What was the effect of Peter Zenger's printing of the articles against the governor?

....

....

3. How does Zenger's actions affect Americans today?

....

....

4. Explain the differences in children's schooling under Dutch and English rule.

....

....

....

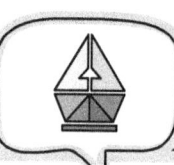

This week you have learned what life was like in the New York colony, both under Dutch and British rule. You learned about the economy, the enslaved Africans, government, and the effects on children in the colony. You also know that the Native Americans were losing more and more of the land that they once lived freely on.

Directions: Read the text below. Then answer the questions that follow.

Write an article for *The New-York Weekly Journal* describing how your life, as either a colonist or a slave, in the colony has changed. Use the information you learned this week to help you include important details.

History

The French and Indian War

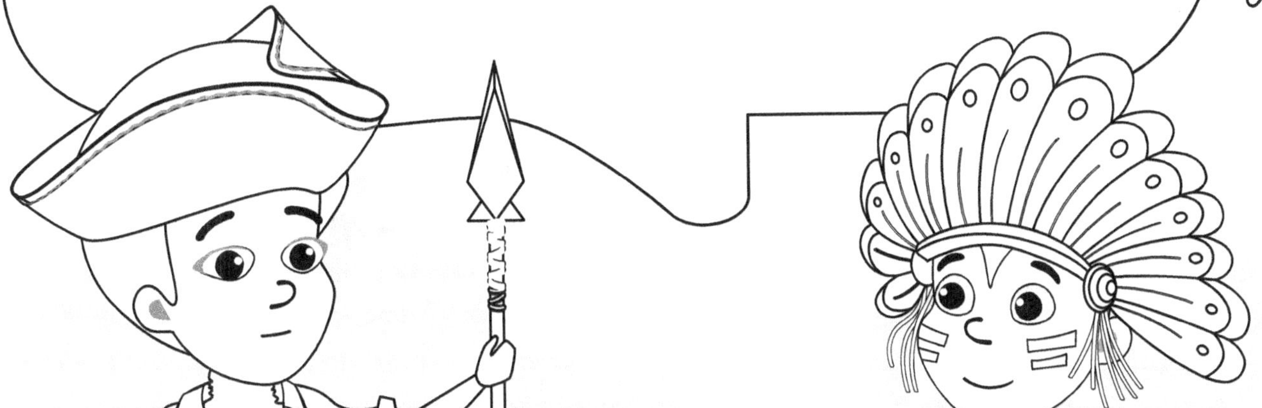

Learn about the events that led to the French and Indian War.

ARGOPREP

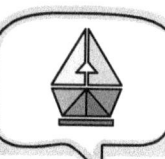
Directions: Read the text below. Then answer the questions that follow.

The area west of the Appalachian Mountains and north of the Ohio River was known as **Ohio Country.** This included Ohio, eastern Indiana, western Pennsylvania, and West Virginia. Use the map above to circle this area.

In the 1600s and 1700s, Ohio Country was claimed to be owned by both **England** and **France.** In 1748, the Ohio Company was formed to profit from the land. The company purchased 200,000 acres of land in the Ohio Country from the King of England and resold it to settlers for a higher price. This proved to be a successful business.

When the French found out that the King of England was selling the land they believed belonged to them, they were furious. The French built a fort in Ohio Country along the Ohio River called **Fort Duquense.** This action caused the first battle of the **French and Indian War** in 1754.

The name of this war can cause confusion. You would think that it was the French and the Indians who were at odds, but it was actually a war between the French and the British. The Native Americans were allies, or partners, with both sides. Different tribes chose a side based on who they believed could help them following the war. The British had the Iroquois, Catawba, and Cherokee tribes on their side. While the French had the Shawnee, Lenape, Ojibwa, Ottawa, and Algonquin tribe as allies.

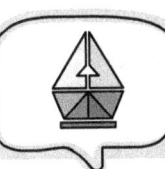
1. Describe where Ohio Country is located.

2. How did the Ohio Company make money?

    A. They sold more land to the King of England.

    B. They sold land for the King of England.

    C. They bought land from the King of England to resell.

    D. They helped the King of England take over Ohio Country.

3. The French and the Indians fought against each other in the "French and Indian War."

    A. True

    B. False

4. Why did the French and Indian War start?

Directions: Read the text below. Then answer the questions that follow.

As you know, the **French and Indian War** began because the French and the British colonists both thought that they had rights to the Ohio Country land. There were three groups involved in the war: the Native Americans from the Ohio Country, the French colonists, and the British colonists. Each group had different motives or reasons, to participate in the French and Indian War.

There were close to 70,000 **French settlers** that lived in Canada, Illinois, and Louisiana. They were partners with the Native Americans and depended on them for crops. The French did not plan to settle in the Ohio Country area, but they wanted to be the only people trading with the Native Americans in the area.

There were more than one million **British colonists** living throughout North America. The British really wanted to land because they were good at farming. The more land they could acquire, the more they had to farm on. They wanted a relationship with the Native Americans so they could continue to trade and get fur.

When the French and Indian War began, there were more than 3,000 **Native Americans** living in Ohio Country. They had moved to the area to escape the British settlements along the coast. They wanted access to land to grow food and hunt. They wanted to keep their options for trading open. By trading their furs, Native Americans were able to get weapons, metal tools, and cloth, such as linen.

1. What were the three groups involved in the French and Indian War?

    A.

    B.

    C.

2. The French wanted the Ohio Country land because...

    A. They wanted to trade with the Native Americans in the area.

    B. They wanted more land than the British.

    C. They wanted to push the Native Americans off the land.

    D. They knew that the Ohio Country would make them money.

3. The British wanted the Ohio Country land because...

    A. They wanted to trade with the Native Americans in the area.

    B. They wanted more land to farm on.

    C. They wanted to become friends with the Native Americans that lived there.

    D. They knew that the Ohio Country would make them money.

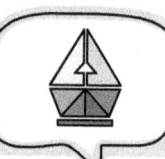
Directions: Read the text below. Then answer the questions that follow.

"

There were several battles that took place in the French and Indian War. Many of them took place in the state of New York. The British had twice as many troops as the French. However, the French used their Native American allies to help them win battles. This worked well for the French at the beginning of the war. However, the British became more successful by the end of the war. After winning at **Fort Niagara** in 1759, the British forced the French to surrender in Quebec.

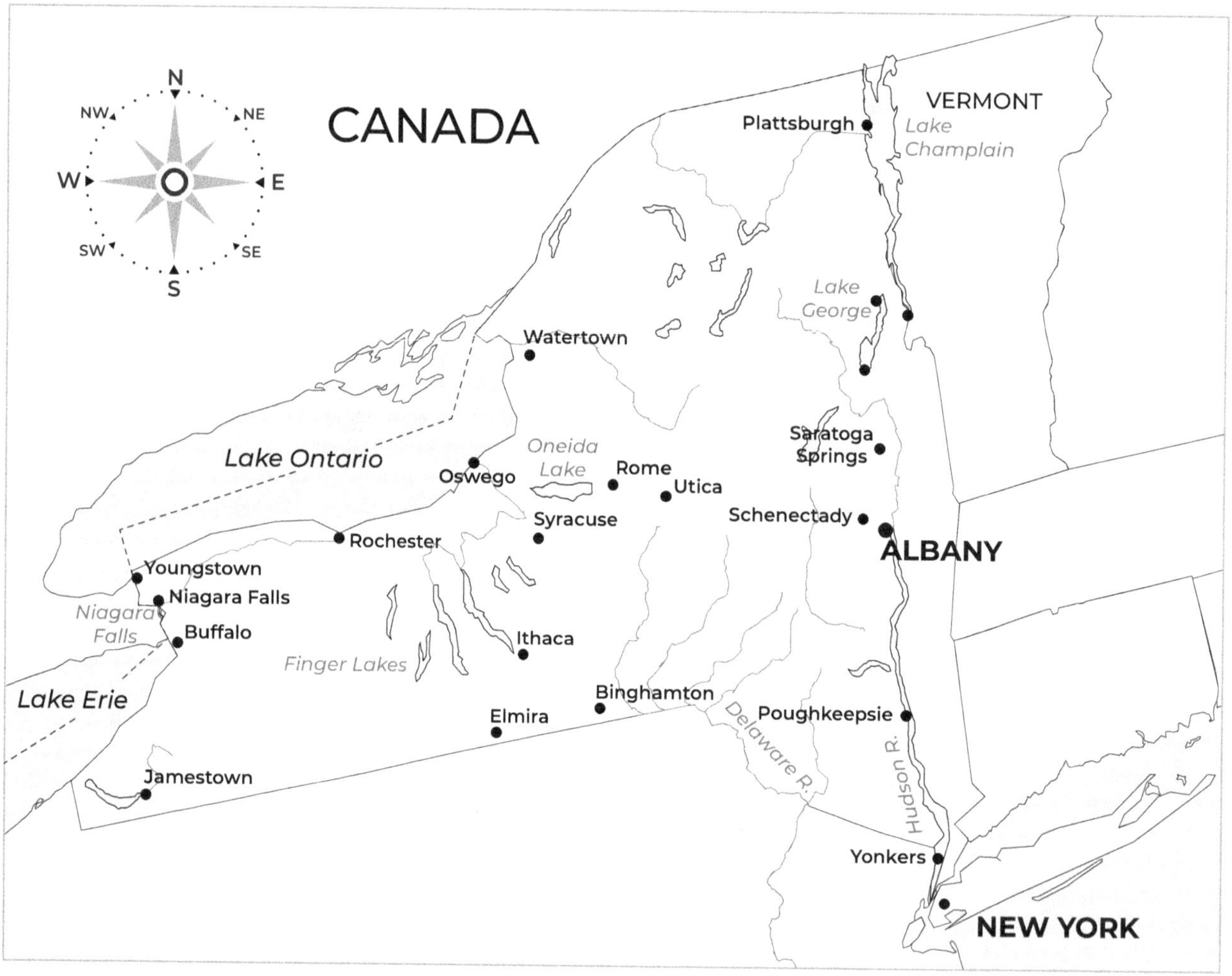

"

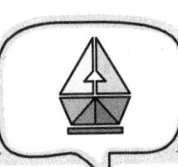
As you read about the battles, mark the locations where they happened on the map of New York.

1. On March 27, 1756, in Rome, New York, the French burned down Fort Bull. The fort was located near the waterway the connects Albany, NY to Lake Ontario. The French won this battle.

2. In August 1756, in Oswego, New York, the French captured the British Fort and forced them to surrender. This is known as the Battle of Fort Oswego.

3. The Massacre at Fort William Henry took place in August 1757 on the southern end of Lake George. The French attacked Fort William Henry, and the British surrendered.

4. On July, 8, 1758, the Battle of Fort Caillon, also known as the Battle of Ticonderoga, occurred. This battle was the deadliest. Over 1,500 British soldiers were killed. This French victory happened at Lake Champlain on the border of New York and Vermont.

5. The Battle on Snowshoes, near Lake George, NY, took place on March 13, 1758. This battle got its name because of the shoes the French were wearing. They won the battle.

6. The French-owned Fort Niagara was seized by the British in July of 1759. This battle, known as the Battle of Fort Niagara, occurred north of Youngstown, NY on the east side of the Niagara River. The loss was significant since the fort was the main supply for other French forts.

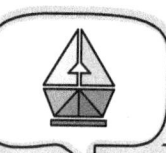
Directions: Read the text below. Then answer the questions that follow.

On February 10, 1763, the **Treaty of Paris** was signed, which ended the French and Indian War. The British had won, and they now controlled the land east of the Mississippi River.

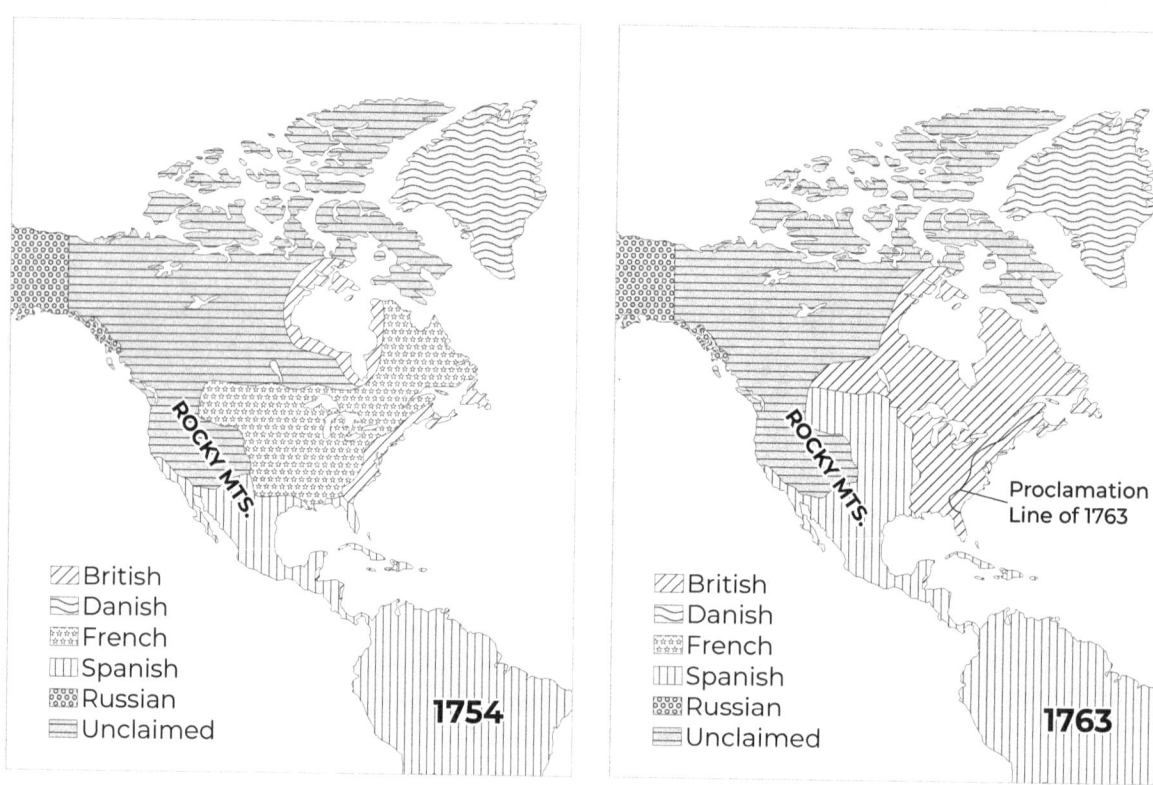

The British now had plenty of land to farm and profit from. However, the war was so expensive that it left the British in a bad place financially. The government decided that to pay for the war, they would **tax** the colonies. The colonists did not want to pay taxes because they could not even be a part of the government. The British felt that taxation was only fair since they had won the land for the colonists to keep.

The colonists were not the only ones who were unhappy with the results of the war. The Native Americans disliked the treaty. They had helped the British win the war and they hadn't received any land in return.

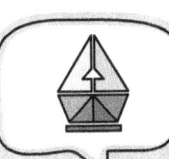
Complete the chart to document how each of the three groups involved in the French and Indian War was impacted by the Treaty of Paris.

The French	Native Americans	The British

Directions: Read the text below. Then answer the questions that follow.

This week you have learned about the **French and Indian War,** which was a series of battles between the French and the British for land in Ohio Country. When the British won the war, the Native Americans who had aligned with the French were very unhappy with the outcome of the war. The British moved them from their land.

Pontiac was the name of the Ottawa tribe's leader. He organized **Pontiac's Rebellion** in 1763. They took control of Fort Detroit and killed the soldiers. They continued to attack British forts and kill their men. The British knew they needed to make peace with the Native Americans. A peace treaty was signed in 1766, with the British agreeing to stay east of the Appalachian Mountains.

1. What was the cause of the French and Indian War?

....

....

2. What was the effect of the French and Indian War?

....

....

3. What was the cause of Pontiac's Rebellion?

....

....

4. What was the effect of Pontiac's Rebellion?

....

....

WEEK 9

History

The Great Divide

Learn about the aftermath of the French and Indian War and how it led to conflicts between American colonists.

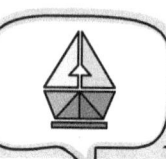
Directions: Read the text below. Then answer the questions that follow.

Last week you learned about the French and Indian War that lasted for nine years. England won, but the country was in debt because of its victory. It was an expensive war to fight. The British troops used the British treasury to pay for it. The British wanted their money back by taxing the colonists. **King George III** was the ruler of England. He believed that the colonists owed them because the war protected their land.

The British passed the **Townsend Acts** in 1767 to get their money from the colonists. These acts taxed goods like paper, glass, and tea. They also passed the **Stamp Act.** This act required all paper used in the colonies to have a special stamp on them. Colonists would have to pay to get this special stamp.

The colonists were not happy about the new acts. They protested, "No taxation without representation." They did not have anyone representing them in the English Parliament. They only wanted to pay taxes that would go their own colonies.

1. Why did the British pass the Townsend Acts?

    A. They wanted to start a war with the colonists.

    B. They wanted to tax the colonists.

    C. They wanted to push the colonists out.

    D. They wanted to pay for the French and Indian War themselves.

2. Why did the British think taxation was fair?

3. Why did the colonists think taxation was unfair?

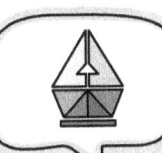
Directions: Read the text below. Then answer the questions that follow.

The colonists were determined to protest the **British taxation.** First, they stopped buying their goods. Next, they formed a group to organize protests and write articles about the British. They called this group the **Sons of Liberty.**

The colonist's boycotting actions began to hurt British businesses. They asked the government to lift the taxes on the colonists. The government agreed to overturn the taxation on everything but tea.

The **East India Company** was suffering financially. The British government passed the **Tea Act** to help the company. The act stated that The East India Company was the only business allowed to sell tea in the colonies. Without competition from other companies, The East India Company was able to offer tea at very low prices.

The Sons of Liberty were not thrilled with the Tea Act. Due to the low price of tea, it was impossible to keep people boycotting it. They were determined to hold their stand on taxation, even if it was only on tea. Therefore, the colonists dressed as Native Americans and went to the Boston harbor where the ships were holding the tea. They went aboard and dumped all the tea into the water. This event, which happened on December 16, 1773, is known as the **Boston Tea Party.**

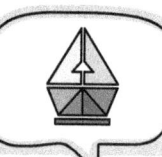
1. Who were the Sons of Liberty?

    A. members of the British government
    B. colonists working at The East India Company
    C. local Native American tribe
    D. colonists boycotting British taxation

2. The colonist's determination paid off and the British government overturned all taxation.

    A. True
    B. False

3. What were the effects of the Tea Act?

4. What was the purpose of the Boston Tea Party?

Directions: Read the text below. Then answer the questions that follow.

Yesterday you learned about the **Boston Tea Party.** The colonists wanted to continue the boycott of the taxation in the colonies and demonstrate their anger about the Tea Act. When King George heard about the colonists dumping the tea in the Boston Harbor, he wanted revenge. Therefore, in 1774, he and his government passed the **Intolerable Acts.** These acts were broken into several action steps all meant to make life hard for the colonists.

First, King George closed the port in Boston. This made it impossible for the colonists to receive goods and supplies from other places. The King refused to reopen the port until the money lost from the overboard tea was repaid.

Next was the **The Quartering Act.** British troops were sent into the colonies to keep order. These soldiers needed housing, meals, and supplies. The colonists were expected to provide these things.

Lastly, the governors who were chosen by the British government were given even more power and influence over the colonies, leaving the colonists with practically no voice. If they had a concern or problem with a governor, they would have to travel all the way to Britain in order to speak out against him.

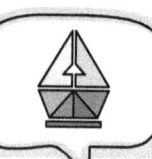
1. How did King George react to the colonist's involvement in the Boston Tea Party?

2. Describe the three main parts of the Intolerable Acts.

   A.

   B.

   C.

3. How do you predict the colonists responded to King George's new acts?

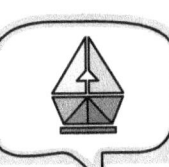
Directions: Read the text below. Then answer the questions that follow.

The constant conflicts between the colonists and England were creating a huge divide. Most of the American colonists were ready to break free from British rule. These colonists were called **patriots.** They did not agree with the lack of representation. Patriots included farmers, craftspeople, and some large landowners. There were some colonists who wanted to remain loyal to the King of England. They did not want independence. These colonists were called **loyalists.** Most were wealthy, professional men. In New York, about half of the population were loyalists.

Since the American colonists were not represented in the current government, a group of men came together to form the **First Continental Congress** in 1774. The men, including George Washington and John Adams, met in Philadelphia to discuss how to respond to the King of England and the Intolerable Acts.

The Congress agreed that the 13 colonies should be an independent country, free from British rule. They decided to form the **Continental Army.** This would be the official army of the colonies. **George Washington** was the chosen leader. In 1775, the British sent soldiers to Massachusetts to disarm the American patriots and arrest the leaders. The Revolutionary War officially began on April 19, 1775 when the **Battles of Lexington and Concord** began.

1. Explain the difference between a patriot and a loyalist.

....

....

....

2. What caused the patriots to form the First Continental Congress?

....

....

....

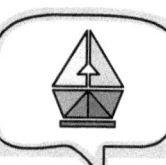
This week you learned about the political and economic issues that caused a divide between the British government and the American colonists. They did not agree on who was responsible for paying the costs of the French and Indian War. However, since the colonists were not represented in the government, they did not have a vote in what was decided. Therefore, they decided to break free from the King of England and his demands. This act of independence started the Revolutionary War.

Directions: Read the text below. Then answer the questions that follow.

Explain the events leading up to the Boston Tea Party and the effects afterward from two different perspectives.

King of England's Perspective   **American Colonist/Patriot's Perspective**

WEEK 10

History

The Revolutionary War

Learn about the events that led to the start of the Revolutionary War and what happened during this historic battle.

Directions: Read the text below. Then answer the questions that follow.

The **American Revolution** was a war in which the 13 colonies fought for their freedom. They wanted to be free from the King of England's rule. Most American colonists were patriots, which meant they supported freedom from Britain. However, some were loyal to the King (loyalists). The patriots formed the **Continental Army**, led by George Washington, to represent the colonies.

The **Battles of Lexington and Concord** (April 1775) launched the war. The British Army wanted to capture rebel leaders, such as **Samuel Adams**, and destroy the Americans' store of weapons and ammunition. However, the colonists were warned by riders, one of whom was **Paul Revere.** The job of a rider was to look out and warn the soldiers when the British were coming. The leaders were able to escape, and the local **militia** (army) was able to hide most of its supplies.

1. The Revolutionary War began because the American colonists wanted to be free from the British government.

    A. True

    B. False

2. Predict what would have happened if the riders had not warned the Continental Army that the British were coming.

Directions: Read the text below. Then answer the questions that follow.

Yesterday you learned about the first battle in the Revolutionary War. The next battle took place in New York, at Fort Ticonderoga. This battle was a huge success for the patriots. A group of soldiers called the **Green Mountain Boys** attacked the British Fort on Lake Champlain. They accessed the fort by rowing across the lake. They were able to capture the fort and several weapons without any bloodshed. The weapons they took would help them in future battles.

After a year of war, the **Second Continental Congress** met again. They decided it was necessary to declare their independence from England. They met on June 11, 1776, to write and sign the **Declaration of Independence.** After writing several drafts and much discussion, the final version of the document was adopted on July 4, 1776. We still celebrate Independence Day as a holiday. Congress sent a copy of the Declaration of Independence to the British government, eager to hear its response.

Britain did not accept the Declaration of Independence. They wanted to keep the colonies under their control. This led to the first major battle of the Revolutionary War: The Battle of Long Island.

1. How did the patriots succeed in capturing Fort Ticonderoga?

    A. They rowed across the lake to the fort.

    B. They decided to not use weapons.

    C. The fort was not owned by the British.

    D. They traded the British weapons for the fort.

2. What was the purpose of the Second Continental Congress meeting?

    A. To plan an attack on the British

    B. To rest from the fighting

    C. To draft the Declaration of Independence

    D. To spy on the British forts

3. How did the British feel about the patriots' Declaration of Independence?

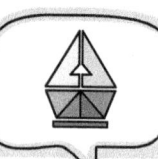
Directions: Read the text below. Then answer the questions that follow.

The government of Britain refused to give the colonists the independence they requested. Instead, its army wanted to capture New York and New York City. The British knew that capturing New York would give them an advantage in the war. New York's geographic location would allow them to create a separation between the northern and southern colonies. New York's harbor also provided a port for the British Navy to easily access. Also, New York had several important waterways.

The British made their move in 1776. First, they took over **Staten Island.** Then, they gained control of **Long Island.** In 1776, Britain took over the entire city of New York. New York City became a retreat for British soldiers and loyalists. Many enslaved people also came. They hoped to gain freedom if Britain won the war.

The British government had a plan to take over New York entirely. They sent three different armies to take over areas along New York's waterways. However, they were stopped by the colonists in the **Battle of Saratoga.** Americans hid in the woods and surprised the enemy. This was a new technique in fighting, and it worked. After two battles, the British surrendered. This battle is considered a turning point in the Revolutionary War.

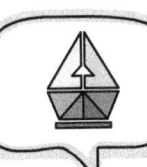
1. What about New York made it a desirable location to take control of?

2. How did the American colonists win the Battle of Saratoga?

3. Why do you think this battle was considered a turning point in the war?

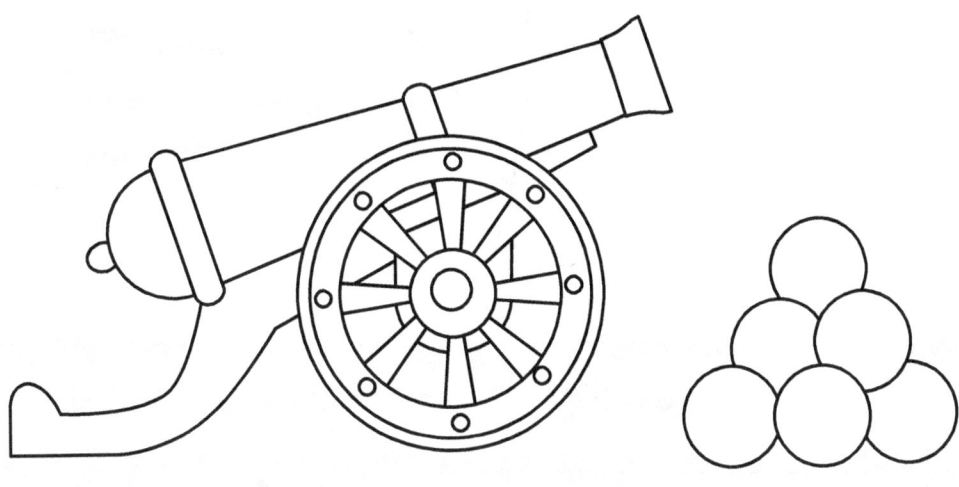

Directions: Read the text below. Then answer the questions that follow.

Yesterday you learned about the **Battle of Saratoga.** This battle was an important one in the Revolutionary War because it is considered the turning point. Up until that point, the British had been very successful in battle. However, the colonists used a different fighting approach at Saratoga and saved New York from being completely overturned by the British. If the British would have won the battle, they would have taken over, and America would have been forced to surrender.

America's win showed France they had a chance against the British. France decided to help out. They still considered Britain an enemy from the French and Indian War, so they sent money, ships, and soldiers.

The final important battle of the war was the **Battle of Yorktown.** French ships and soldiers helped Washington's army surround the British, and they were forced to surrender. In 1783, the British and the American leaders signed the **Treaty of Paris.** The peace treaty declared the official end of the Revolutionary War and granted the patriots their desired independence.

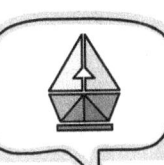
1. Why was the Battle of Saratoga considered to be the turning point of the war?

....

....

....

....

2. What were two effects of the Battle of Saratoga?

....

....

....

3. Why was France willing to help the American colonists?

....

....

....

....

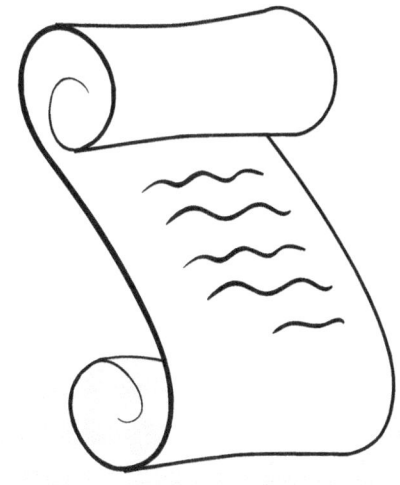

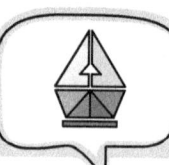
Directions: Read the text below. Then answer the questions that follow.

"

This week you learned about the events leading up to the Revolutionary War and the battles that took place. You know that America, led by Washington's army, won the war. When the peace treaty was signed in Paris, France on September 3, 1783, there were some important takeaways for the colonies.

The treaty restored peace between Britain and the colonies.

Britain lost control of the land and government of the thirteen colonies.

The thirteen colonies were now considered free and independent states.

Colonists were given the freedom to expand the country west if they wanted to.

"

Explain how the Revolutionary War affects how and where we live today. Think: How would the country and state be different if the colonists surrendered to the British soldiers? How would American freedoms be different? Use the information you learned in the past two weeks to support your thinking.

....

....

....

....

....

....

....

....

WEEK 11

Civics and Government

A New Government

Discover how the Revolutionary War led to the birth of a new government in America.

ARGOPREP

Directions: Read the text below. Then answer the questions that follow.

Last week, you learned about **The Revolutionary War.** Remember this war was started by American colonists who wanted freedom from British rulers. The Declaration of Independence, The Treaty of Paris, and victorious battles eventually led to their freedom. Now, colonists were able to form their own government.

The **Constitution** of The United States was the foundation of the new government. It would serve as the supreme law of America, outlining the rights of American citizens. As former colonies began to form state governments, they appointed **delegates** to attend the Constitutional Convention in 1787. These delegates spoke on behalf of the states to make decisions about the new American government. There were originally 70 delegates, though only 55 were able to go to the convention in Philadelphia. Of those 55, only 39 delegates signed the Constitution on September 17, 1787. These delegates are known as the **framers** of the Constitution. Framers such as George Washington, Alexander Hamilton, and Benjamin Franklin are called the **Founding Fathers** of America. Their leadership helped to create a strong government for American citizens.

1. Why was the Constitution an important part of the new American government?

   A. It served as the supreme law of the United States.

   B. It outlined the rights of American citizens.

   C. It was the foundation of the new government.

   D. All of these reasons

2. Who did the states appoint to go to the Constitutional Convention?

   A. soldiers

   B. framers

   C. delegates

   D. treaties

3. Explain why some framers are called the Founding Fathers of America.

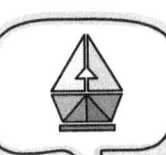
Yesterday you learned about the foundation of the American government. You know that the Constitution was written as the supreme law of America. It gave Americans new rights, since they were no longer under British law. Today you will learn more about the Constitution and what it means.

Directions: Read the text below. Then answer the questions that follow.

The **Preamble** is the introduction of the Constitution. It explains the reason why the Constitution was written. The Preamble states:

"We the People of the United States, in Order to form a more perfect Union, establish Justice, insure domestic Tranquility, provide for the common defense, promote the general Welfare, and secure the Blessings of Liberty to ourselves and our Posterity, do ordain and establish this Constitution for the United States of America."

In 1791, **The Bill of Rights** was added to the Constitution. These 10 **amendments**, or changes, gave Americans more specific rights. They include freedom of speech, freedom of religion, and fair trials in court. Over the years, more amendments have been added to the Constitution. There are now a total of 27 amendments.

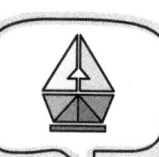
1. The Preamble is the   of the Constitution.

   A. introduction

   B. conclusion

   C. amendment

   D. replacement

2. Explain why The Bill of Rights was added to the Constitution.

Directions: Read the text below. Then answer the questions that follow.

"

Remember that the Constitution was written as the supreme law of America. It not only served as the law for citizens but for American leaders as well. The Constitution made sure that leaders did not have too much power.

You know that George Washington was an army leader and a Founding Father of America. In 1789, he became the first **President of the United States.** Washington did not want to be like British kings. He did not want to have all of the power. Washington started appointing other leaders and called them the **Presidential Cabinet.** The Cabinet consisted of leaders such as the Supreme Court Chief Justice, Secretary of State and Secretary of War. President Washington talked to his cabinet about important decisions regarding the country.

The Constitution allows presidents to choose Cabinet members. Presidents also have the power to:

declare war

send troops to battle

have important meetings with world leaders

make treaties

vote on laws

decide how America's money is spent

"

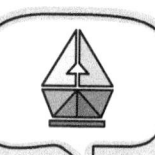
1. Why didn't George Washington want to have all the power as President?

2. List 3 powers that presidents have according to the Constitution.

Directions: Read the text below. Then answer the questions that follow.

"

You know the Constitution was the foundation of the new American government. It outlines laws and rights for citizens. The Constitution also gave the President certain powers but made sure they don't have too much power.

"

Today you will read the Constitution. You can find a copy on websites such as archives. gov. Write a paragraph about something you learned. Explain why you think this information is important.

_____

_____

_____

_____

_____

_____

_____

_____

_____

_____

_____

_____

Directions: Read the text below. Then answer the questions that follow.

This week you learned how the American government was started. Today you will create a timeline. Think about the events that led to a new government in America. Put them in order below.

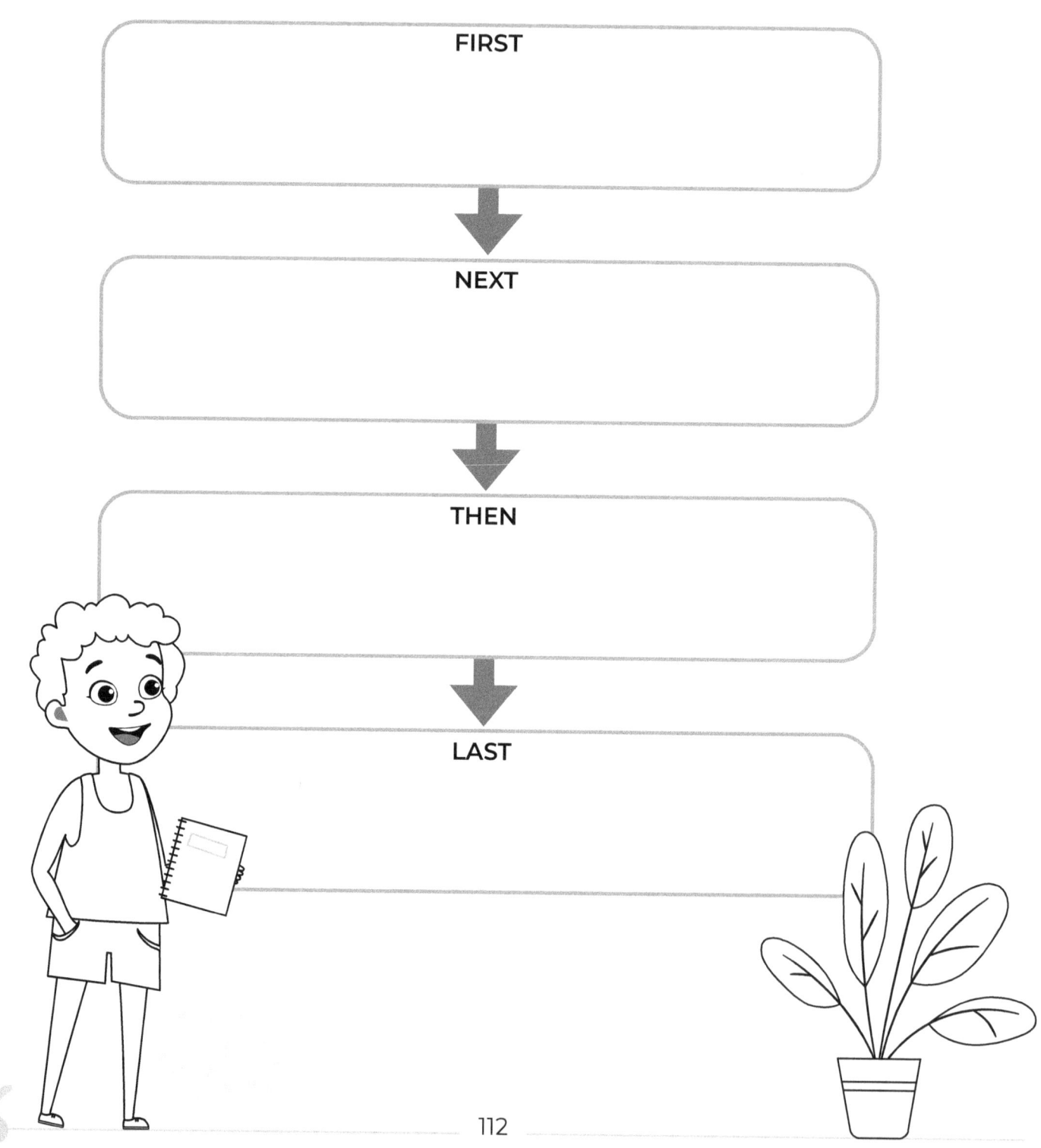

FIRST

NEXT

THEN

LAST

WEEK 12

Civics and Government

Three Branches of Government

Learn about the purpose and functions of the three government branches in America.

ARGOPREP

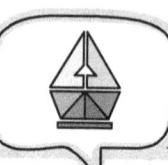
Directions: Read the text below. Then answer the questions that follow.

Last week, you learned about the start of a new government in America. You know that George Washington was the first President of the United States. The Constitution gave him certain powers. He appointed Cabinet members to help him lead the country.

Remember that Americans did not want government leaders to have too much power. One solution was to divide the government into three branches: **executive**, **legislative** and **judicial**. Members of each branch have different powers. The **President** is part of the executive branch which enforces laws. But first, these laws are made by the legislative branch. **Congress** members are part of the legislative branch. A group of judges from the **judicial branch** evaluate the laws. Judges make sure that the laws are fair.

3 Branches of Government

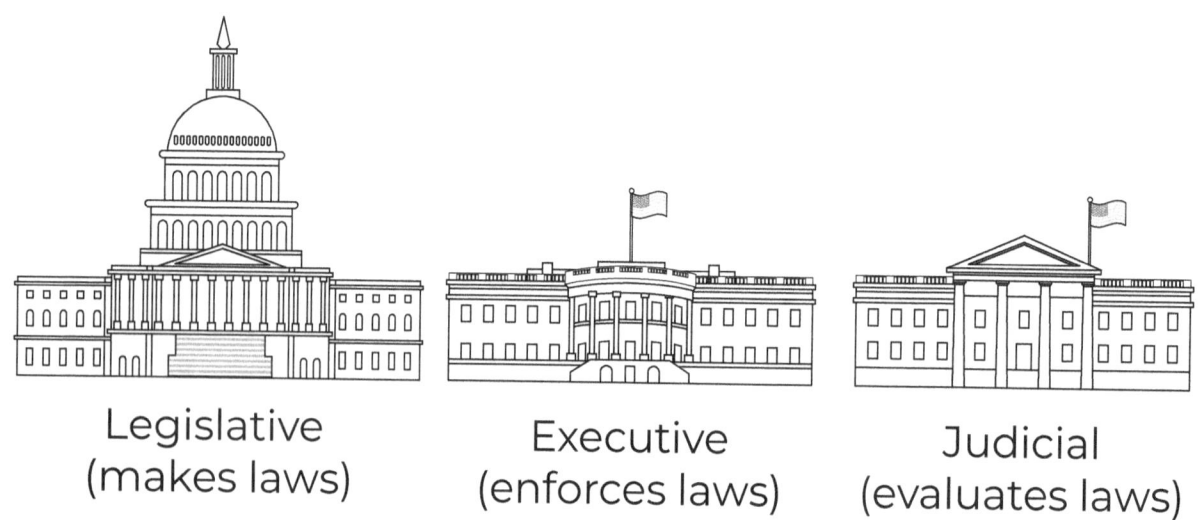

Legislative
(makes laws)

Executive
(enforces laws)

Judicial
(evaluates laws)

1. Why was the American government divided into 3 branches?

   A. There were too many leaders to fit in one building.

   B. To ensure that no leader had too much power.

   C. American leaders did not get along with one another.

   D. The President wanted a new set of powers.

2. Explain how each branch has different roles and powers.

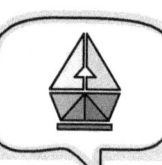
Yesterday you learned about the three branches of government in America. Each branch has different powers. They all take part in the lawmaking process. Today you will learn more about how that process works.

Directions: Read the text below. Then answer the questions that follow.

" Remember that laws begin in the legislative branch. They start off as ideas and become **bills**. Congress members then vote on these bills. In America, Congress has two parts: the **Senate** and the **House of Representatives**. Both parts must agree on a bill. If they do, the bill is sent to the executive branch. The President can sign the bill or **veto** it. When a bill is vetoed, it is rejected and does not become a law. If the bill is signed and becomes a law, the judicial branch will then evaluate it. A group of judges will make sure that the law is fair. "

```
Ideas become bills
        ↓
Congress votes on the bill
        ↓
If members of both the House and the Senate
agree, they send the bill to the President
        ↓
The President signs the bill
        ↓
The bill becomes a law
```

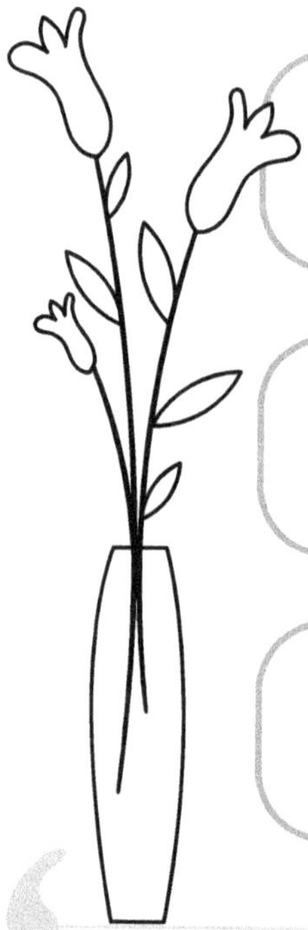

1. Which of these steps in the lawmaking process happens first?

    A. The President signs bills.

    B. Congress members vote on bills.

    C. Judges decide if a law is fair.

    D. A bill is sent to the executive branch.

2. True or false?

Both the House of Representatives and the Senate must agree on a bill before they send it to the President.

    A. true

    B. false

3. What happens when a bill is vetoed?

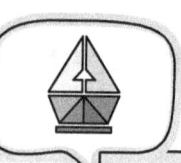
Yesterday you learned how laws are made in America. You know that all 3 government branches play a role in the lawmaking process. Each branch also has different powers. Today you will learn more about those powers

Directions: Read the text below. Then answer the questions that follow.

Government Branch	Powers
Legislative (Congress)	can decide who should be nominated as leaders (presidents, Supreme Court judges, etc.) can declare war can make changes to old laws or create new ones
Executive (President)	is the leader of the United States is the Commander-in-Chief and is in charge of the U.S. military forces can choose Cabinet members
Judicial (Supreme Court)	is the highest court in America can decide if laws violate Constitutional rights can decide if someone is guilty of breaking a law

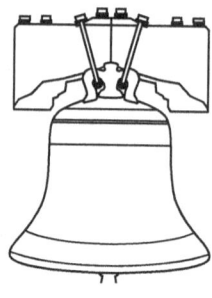

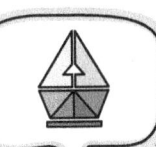
1. Which of these is a power of the legislative branch?

   A. choosing Cabinet members

   B. deciding if someone has broken a law

   C. leading the U.S. army

   D. changing old laws

2. Which of these is NOT a presidential power of the executive branch?

   A. deciding if laws violate the Constitution

   B. being a Commander-in-Chief

   C. choosing Cabinet members

   D. leading the country

3. True or false?

The Supreme Court is among the lowest level of courts in America.

   A. true

   B. false

4. Explain why the Constitution gives each government branch separate powers.

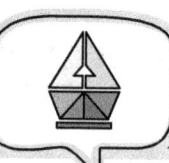
Directions: Read the text below. Then answer the questions that follow.

Remember that each branch of government plays a part in the lawmaking process. Laws start as ideas from citizens or leaders. Today you will think of a new law. Pretend that you want to present your idea to Congress. Use resources such as the Internet to find out how you could do this. Explain the process below.

Directions: Read the text below. Then answer the questions that follow.

This week you learned about the three branches of American government. Today you will review what you have learned. Label the chart below and write three things that you learned about each branch.

Three Branches of Government

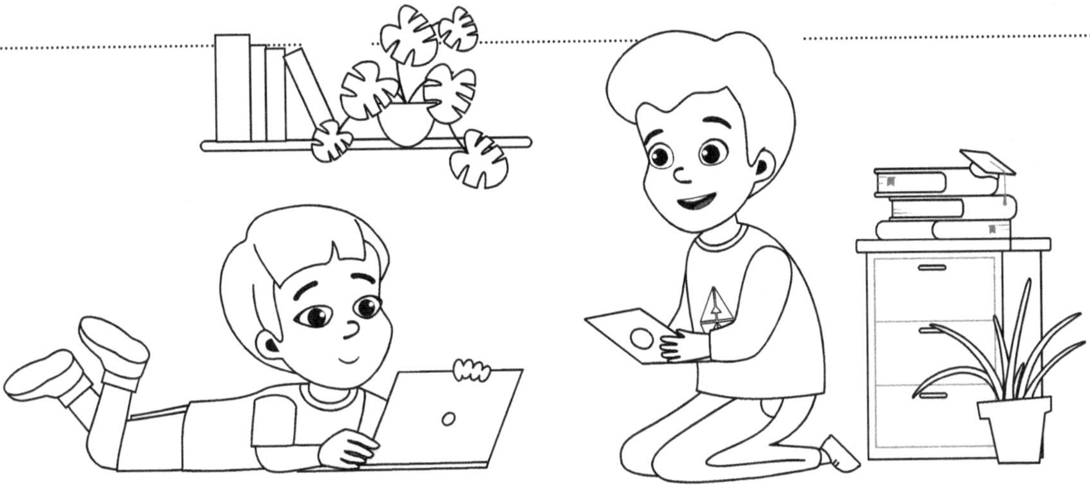

WEEK 13

Civics and Government

State Government

Explore the similarities and differences between state and national government in America.

ARGOPREP

Directions: Read the text below. Then answer the questions that follow.

You have learned about the American government over the past few weeks. You know that it started with the **Constitution.** You also know that there are 3 branches of government in America. Each branch has different roles and powers. This week, you will learn more about state governments. They are very similar to the national government system in America.

Remember that the Constitution gave American leaders certain powers. It also gave American citizens special rights. The **10th Amendment** grants some powers to state leaders. It says:

"The powers not delegated to the United States by the Constitution, nor prohibited by it to the States, are reserved to the States respectively, or to the people."

This means that state governments can make decisions about laws and rights in their local communities. Each state even has its own Constitution. However, local laws and rights cannot violate the U.S. Constitution.

1. Which amendment grants powers to state government leaders?

   A. 22nd

   B. 5th

   C. 10th

   D. 16th

2. Each state has its own ....

   A. government

   B. leader

   C. Constitution

   D. all of these

3. True or false?

   State governments follow their own Constitution, not the U.S. Constitution.

   A. true

   B. false

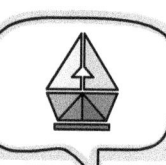
Yesterday you learned about state governments. The Constitution allows states to have their own laws, rights, and Constitutions. Remember that states must also follow the U.S. Constitution. This week you will learn how state governments work. Let's take a closer look at the New York state government.

Directions: Read the text below. Then answer the questions that follow.

"

The **Constitution of New York** was first written in 1777. It has undergone many changes over the years. The final version, which was written in 1938, is still used to govern the state of New York today. Like the U.S. Constitution, the New York State Constitution outlines laws and rights for state citizens. It also has a Preamble, a Bill of Rights, and Articles. One of the main differences is that a state Constitution addresses local laws as well. These laws include areas such agriculture, transportation, and labor.

The state of New York is led by a **governor** who enforces state laws. The governor also makes decisions about taxes, education, the environment and other important issues in New York. The governor oversees special departments such as the Department of Taxation and Finance, the Department of Health and the Department of Transportation.

"

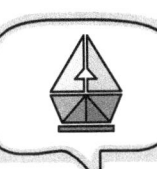
1. Describe how the U.S. government is similar to the local state governments.

2. What is the main difference between the New York State Constitution and the U.S. Constitution?

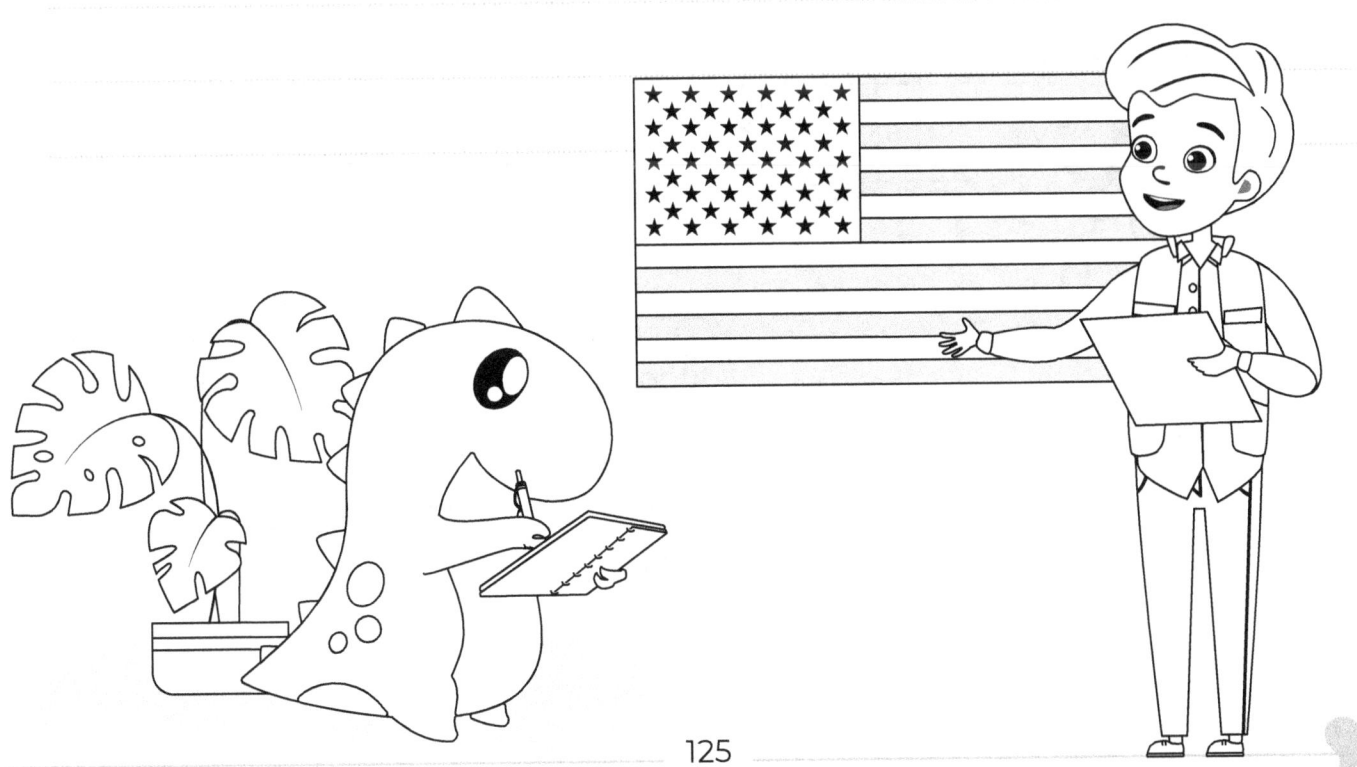

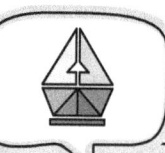
Directions: Read the text below. Then answer the questions that follow.

You know that the U.S. government has 3 branches. Did you know that states also have 3 branches of government? Today you will learn more about the 3 branches of New York.

The **legislative branch** of New York makes the laws. It is a **bicameral system.** This means that it has two parts: the **Senate** and the **Assembly.** They are led by a senator and an assemblyman. This branch makes decisions about government funds, state leaders, and court judges.

The **executive branch** of New York is led by the Governor. The Governor is the Commander-in-Chief of the state. Some other responsibilities include budgeting the state's money, vetoing bills, and appointing state officers. The Lieutenant Governor, the State Comptroller, and the Attorney General are also leaders in the executive branch.

The **judicial branch** of New York consists of judges in the Court of Appeals. It is led by the Chief Judge. The judicial branch makes decisions about local cases. Judges also make sure that laws in New York are fair according to the Constitution.

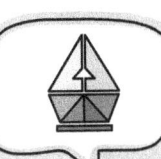

Think about what you learned about the 3 branches of New York state government. Write a few facts about each branch in the table below.

Legislative	Executive	Judicial

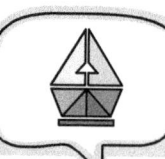
Yesterday you learned about the New York state government. Today you will research information about your own state government. Note: If you live in New York, you will look for specific details about its current government.

Directions: Read the text below. Then answer the questions that follow.

1. What state do you live in?

2. Who is the governor of your state?

3. List 3 more government leaders in your state.

4. What did you learn about the government branches in your state?

This week you learned about the government system in states such as New York. Today you will review some key vocabulary terms for state governments.

Directions: Look at each term and write the definition on the line.

1. bicameral ....

....

2. senator ....

....

3. assemblyman..

....

4. governor ....

....

5. True or false?

The Lieutenant Governor is a leader in the judicial branch of New York.

   A. true
   B. false

6. True or false?

The Court of Appeals is led by the Chief Judge in New York.

   A. true
   B. false

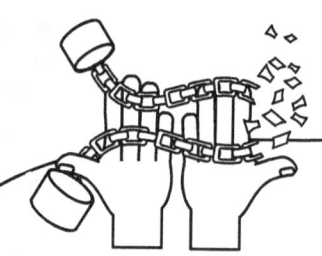

Civics and Government

Human Rights

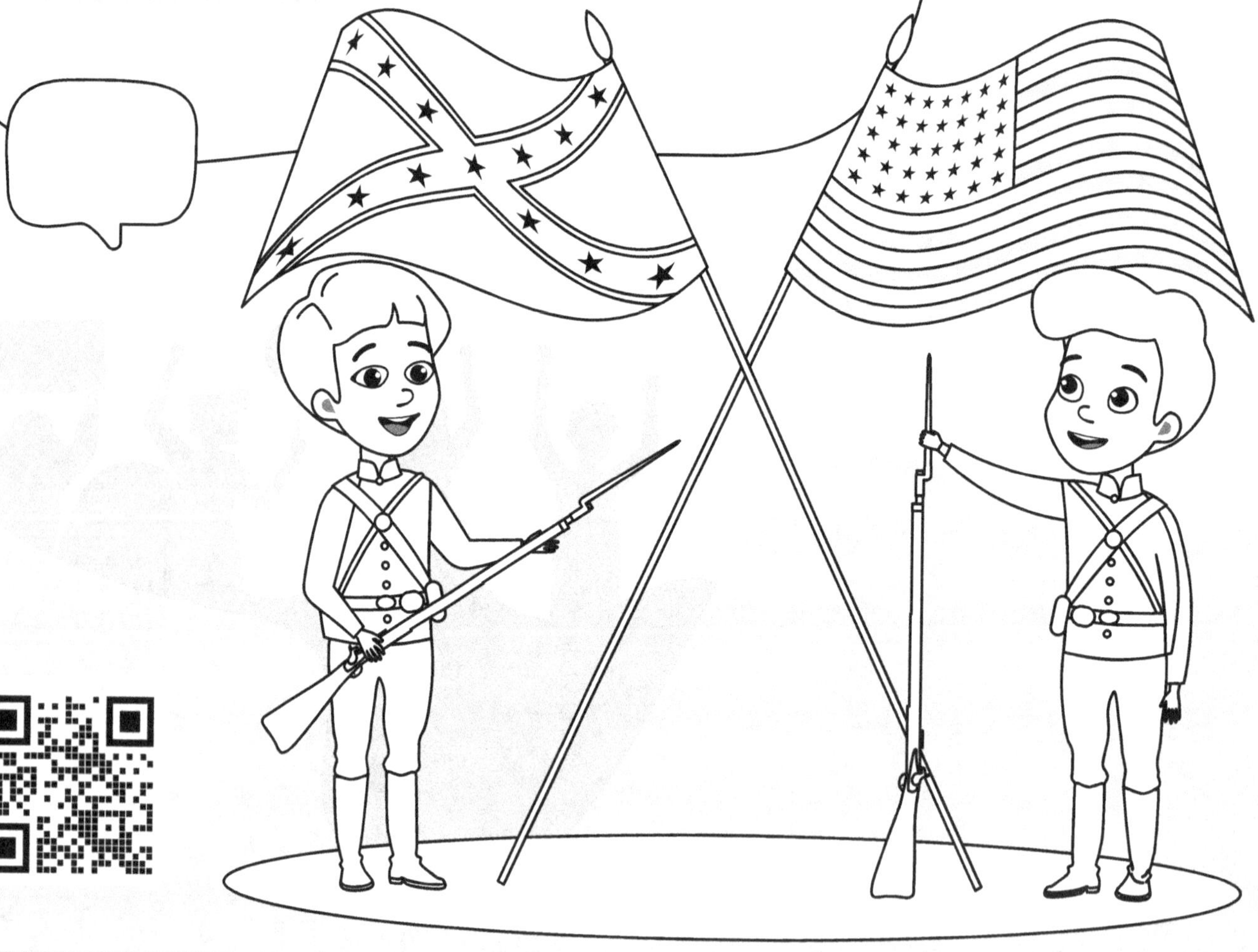

Learn about the history of inequality and those who fought for human rights in America.

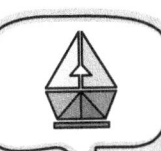
*You have learned about the Constitutional rights of American citizens. You know that Constitutions, both national and local, were written to give people these rights. But many years ago, some people did not have the same rights in America as other people. This week you will learn about people who fought for equality and **human rights**.*

Directions: Read the text below. Then answer the questions that follow.

"

Remember that America gained its independence from Great Britain in the 1700s. The **Constitution** and the **Bill of Rights** were written to guarantee freedom for American citizens. However, during this time many African-Americans were forced to work as slaves. They did not have the same rights as free white men. In the 1800s, **abolitionists** started a movement to end slavery. Fredrick Douglass, Harriet Tubman, William Lloyd Garrison and other abolitionists were leaders in this movement.

The quest to end slavery in America was not easy. There were many people, mainly in the South, who did not want to abolish slavery. They relied on slaves to grow crops such as cotton and tobacco. They thought that if slavery ended, it would cause many people to lose the money they made from selling crops. Crops were not a major concern in the North, where people made more money from factories than farming. Plus, times were changing. People started to form new opinions about moral and legal issues regarding slavery.

"

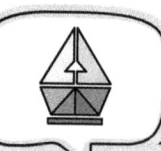
1. What was the main goal for abolitionists?

    A. to write a new Constitution

    B. to end slavery in America

    C. to grow more crops in the South

    D. to build factories in the North

2. Why did some people in the South want slavery to continue?

    A. They did not want to lose money.

    B. They wanted to move further North.

    C. They wanted to grow their own crops.

    D. They did not want slavery to continue.

3. Explain why slavery was not a major concern for people in Northern states.

Directions: Read the text below. Then answer the questions that follow.

" Yesterday you learned about slavery in America. You know that abolitionists wanted to end slavery. This caused problems between people who did not want slavery to end and those who supported abolitionism. The disagreements were primarily between Northerners and Southerners. This conflict eventually led to the **Civil War** in 1862.

Southern states strongly opposed the abolishment of slavery. When Abraham Lincoln was elected as the 16th President in 1860, he caused even more conflicts. Many Southerners were angry because Lincoln was against slavery. They decided to **secede**, or seperate themselves, and form their own country. This new country would be called **The Confederate States of America.** Meanwhile, the Northern states called themselves the **Union.**

The war began on April 12, 1861 when Southerners fired the first shots at Fort Sumter. The Civil War continued for several years. In 1863, Lincoln introduced the **Emancipation Proclamation** which granted freedom to the slaves. In 1865, the South surrendered. Earlier that year, the 13th Amendment outlawed slavery in America. "

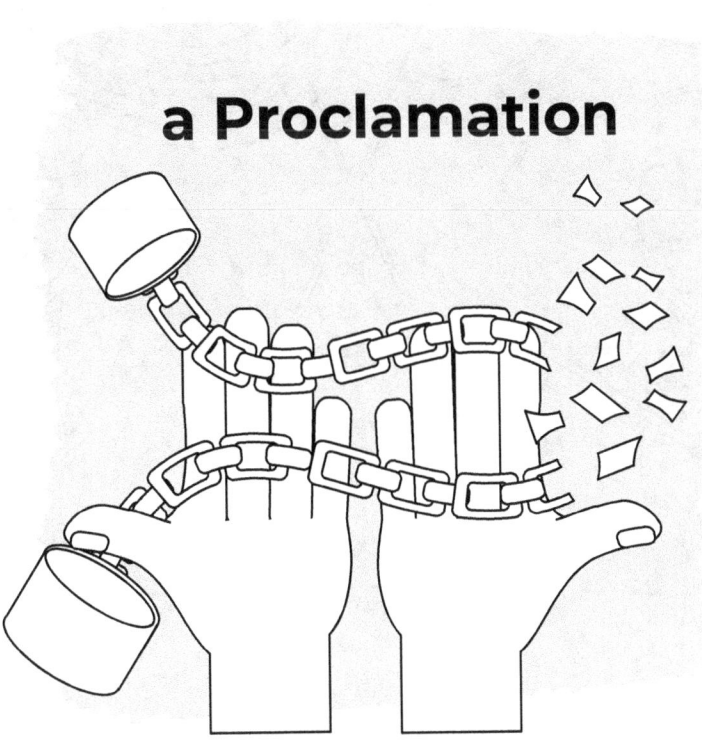

a Proclamation

1. What happened when the South seceded?

   A. They joined forces with the North.
   B. They were led by Abraham Lincoln.
   C. They formed their own country.
   D. They ended the Civil War.

2. What caused the end of the Civil War?

   A. Abraham Lincoln stopped the battle.
   B. There was a battle at Fort Sumter.
   C. The South surrendered.
   D. The 13th Amendment ended the battle.

3. True or false?

   The Emancipation Proclamation and the 13th Amendment ended slavery in America.

   A. true
   B. false

Directions: Read the text below. Then answer the questions that follow.

Yesterday you learned about the Civil War and the end of slavery in America. You know this was a victory for abolitionists who wanted equal rights for all citizens. During this time, African-Americans were not the only ones fighting for human rights. Women in America did not have the same rights as men. Today you will learn about the **Women's Suffrage Movement.**

The Women's Suffrage Movement began in the 1800s. It was led by **activists** such as Elizabeth Cady Stanton and Susan B. Anthony. These activists worked hard to create change in society. They believed that men and women were equal and should have the same rights. In 1848, they held a large meeting to discuss their plans. It was called the **Seneca Falls Convention.** Activists also had parades to gain attention from lawmakers. The Women's Suffrage Movement went on for many years. This later led to the 19th amendment, which gave women the right to vote in 1920.

1. What strategies did activists use to create changes during the Women's Suffrage Movement?

2. What did slaves and white American women have in common during the 1800s?

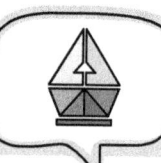
Yesterday you learned about the Women's Suffrage Movement. You know that activists worked hard to gain equal rights for women in America. Today you will learn about the **Civil Rights Movement**. *Like activists who fought for women's rights in the 1800s, civil rights activists wanted equality for African-Americans in the 1950's and 60's.*

Directions: Read the text below. Then answer the questions that follow.

Use resources such as the Internet, books, and videos to learn more about the Civil Rights Movement. Write a brief summary of this movement below. What led to the Civil Rights Movement? Who were the key leaders? What was the outcome?

This week you have learned about human rights in American history. You know that some people did not always have the same rights. Today you will read the words of activists who helped to gain equal rights for all Americans.

Directions: Read the text below. Then answer the questions that follow.

"There shall never be another season of silence until women have the same rights men have on this green earth." - Susan B. Anthony, Women's suffrage activist.

"Without a struggle, there can be no progress." - Frederick Douglass, Former slave and abolitionist.

"I have a dream that my four little children will one day live in a nation where they will not be judged by the color of their skin, but by the content of their character." - Martin Luther King Jr., Civil rights leader.

1. How do you think these leaders felt about equal rights? How do these quotes demonstrate the speaker's thoughts and feelings?

....

....

....

....

....

....

....

....

WEEK 15

Civics and Government

Migration in America

Discover how events such as the Civil War and the end of slavery led to migration in America.

ARGOPREP

You have learned about many changes throughout American history. You know that events, such as wars and activist movements, led to these changes. Today you will learn more about how the American population has changed over time.

Directions: Read the text below. Then answer the questions that follow.

After the Civil War, many Americans started to **migrate** West. When people migrate, they move from one place to another. Remember that since slavery had ended, people were looking for ways to make money. Many people moved to Western states such as California in search of gold. There were also more opportunities to grow crops and open new businesses in the West.

People also moved West to find **bison.** They sold bison fur, skin, and meat. Unfortunately, bison were a main source of survival for Native Americas living in the West. Also, people hunted and killed a large number of bison, not only for money, but for sport. Increased hunting caused the species to become nearly extinct, dropping the population from millions to fewer than 1,000.

1. What does migrate mean?

   A. to move from one place to another

   B. to surrender to your enemies in a battle

   C. to build new homes in your community

   D. to live in the same place for many years

2. Why did people move West after the Civil War?

   A. They were banned from living in the South.

   B. They could make more money in the West

   C. They could own slaves in the West.

   D. They wanted to live closer to their families.

3. What were the pros and cons of selling bison?

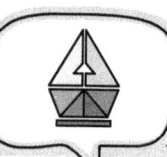
Yesterday you learned about migration after the Civil War. You know that people moved to the Western region to make more money. Today you will learn more about how they traveled.

Directions: Read the text below. Then answer the questions that follow.

People used various trails to travel from their homes to a new life in the West. The main route was the **Oregon Trail,** though there were other trails taken as well. People also used routes such as the **California Trail** and the **Sante Fe Trail.** They mainly traveled in covered wagons pulled by oxen. Though the oxen were strong enough to carry loaded wagons, they were not very fast. It could take months for travelers to complete their journey.

Trails West

1. Which trail do you think took the longest to travel?

2. What was the best trail for people traveling from Illinois to Utah?

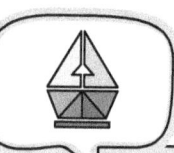
Yesterday you learned about the trails that were used during Western migration in America. You know that people started to move West after the Civil War. Remember that slavery ended around this time as well. So what happened to American slaves once they gained freedom?

Directions: Read the text below. Then answer the questions that follow.

After the Civil War, former slaves began to try and live a normal life in America. This time period was called the **Reconstruction Era.** The South would now rejoin the North as part of the United States. While some moved North, many African-Americans stayed in the South. Although they were free, it was difficult for many to find success due to discrimination and **segregation**. Many former slave owners and supporters of slavery still opposed the idea of African-Americans being a part of society. They believed that black and white people should still live and work in separate communities. However, many African-Americans had limited access to good education and jobs. As a result, they were forced to live in poverty rather than live the abundant life they expected as free citizens.

Years later, many African-Americans grew tired of life in the South. In 1916, **The Great Migration** began. Throughout this period, millions of African-Americans moved to Northern regions such as Chicago and New York City. Since segregation was not legal in the North, African-Americans had more opportunities for jobs and housing. The Great Migration continued for decades as more African-Americans moved from the South to the North.

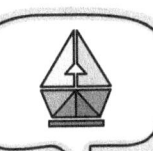
1. Why did former slaves have a hard time starting a new life in the South?

    A. They faced discrimination from those who supported slavery.

    B. Segregation laws banned them from living and working in certain places.

    C. They had limited access to education and jobs.

    D. all of these reasons

2. What was segregation?

    A. the idea that blacks and whites should live separately

    B. the idea that all citizens should have the same rights

    C. the idea that slavery should be abolished

    D. the idea that the South was better than the North

3. True or false?

African-Americans found more opportunities by moving North.

    A. true

    B. false

Yesterday you learned about the Great Migration. Many African-Americans left the South to look for a better life in Northern regions. You know that people migrated from one place to another for different reasons. Today you will compare and contrast these reasons.

Directions: Read the text below. Then answer the questions that follow.

Western migration   **The Great Migration**

This week, you have learned about migration in America. Today you will review what you have learned.

Directions: Read the text below. Then answer the questions that follow.

1. Which of these was NOT one of the trails used to travel West ?

   A. Oregon Trail

   B. Sante Fe Trail

   C. California Trail

   D. British Trail

2. How long did The Great Migration last?

   A. for a few years

   B. for several decades

   C. for three days

   D. for one decade

3. True or false?

   The South rejoined the United States during the Reconstruction Era.

   A. true

   B. false

4. List 3 reasons why African-Americans moved North in the 1900s.

....

....

....

....

WEEK 16

Economics
Industrialization

Learn about the history of industrialization in America and how it affected the way people live and work.

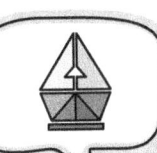
Directions: Read the text below. Then answer the questions that follow.

Last week, you learned about migration in America. You know that many people moved to new places after the Civil War. Life in America continued to change over the years. This week you will learn about **industrialization** in America. This is when jobs that were mainly done by people could now be done by machines. Small jobs could be handled in large factories rather than by one person.

Remember that most farming jobs in the South were once worked by slaves. After slavery ended, the agriculture industry need to find new ways to get jobs done. Some tools such as the cotton gin and the steel plow had already helped make farming easier. Now, new inventions like steam tractors, corn strippers, and cream separators could help farmers get large jobs done more quickly.

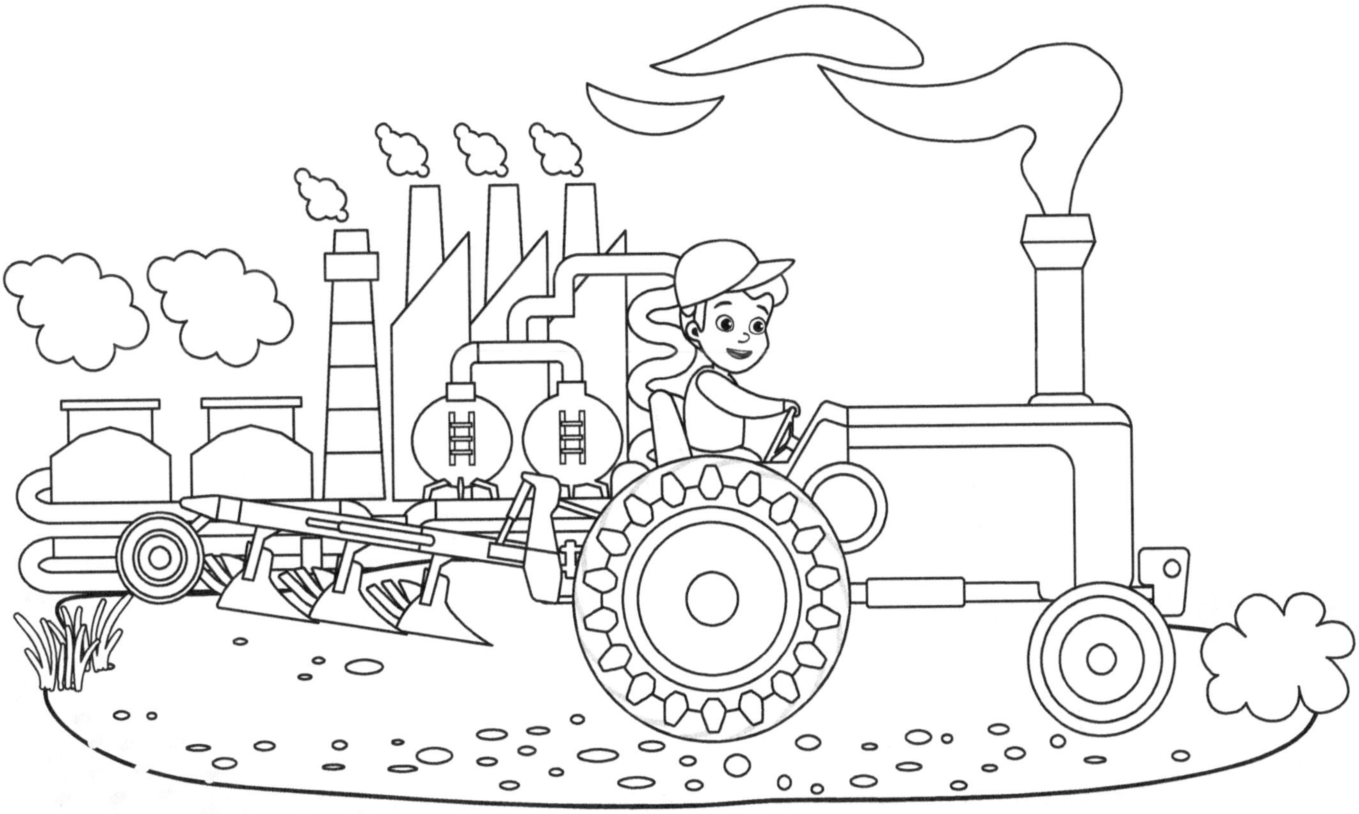

1. What is industrialization?

    A. when people need to move to another place

    B. when machines can do jobs for people

    C. when people buy more farmland to grow crops

    D. when people do jobs by hand instead of machines

2. True or false?

The end of slavery made farming easier for people in the South.

    A. true

    B. false

3. Explain how new farming machines and tools made jobs easier.

Yesterday you learned about industrialization in the American farming industry. Jobs that were once done by hand could now be handled by machines and special tools. Today you will learn about more inventions that changed the way people lived and worked in America.

Directions: Read the text below. Then answer the questions that follow.

From the late 1800s into the early 1900s, technology continued to evolve. Inventors found new ways to make tasks easier. Look at each invention below. Think about how it made life easier for people. Explain in the column on the right.

Invention	How did it make life easier?
telephone	
light bulb	
washing machine	
vacuum cleaner	

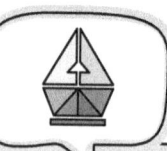
Directions: Read the text below. Then answer the questions that follow.

Remember that factories were a major part of industrialization in America. Small jobs could now be completed by machines or large groups of workers. Today you will learn more about how **factories** changed the way people worked in America.

By the late 1800s, many people began to use factories to save time. They could produce several items, such as clothing and tools, all at once. This was called **mass production.** For example, machines could cut fabric, sew, knit, etc. much faster than human hands. In the amount of time that it would take a person to make one garment, a machine could make many. At this rate, factories could now produce millions of items.

Because mass production saved time, it also saved money. Companies were able to greatly reduce their labor costs. They could hire fewer workers and pay for fewer hours. Plus, companies were able to lower the prices of their items, which helped customers save money as well.

1. What is mass production?

    A. buying several items at the same time

    B. hiring a few workers to make several items

    C. making several items at the same time

    D. selling a few items at a higher price

2. True or false?

Machines could not do certain tasks, like sewing, faster than a human.

    A. true

    B. false

3. How did factories help people save time and money?

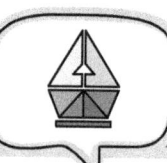
You have learned about how inventions made life and work easier in America. Today you will think about the tasks that you do every day. Some of the things that you use, like a dishwasher, toaster, or hair dryer, did not exist many years ago. How do you think people lived before these inventions?

Directions: Read the text below. Then answer the questions that follow.

Write 3 machines, tools, or items that you use for daily tasks on the left. Explain how people may have completed these tasks before these things were invented. Use resources such as books, the Internet, etc. as needed.

Invention	How did people live before this invention?

Directions: Read the text below. Then answer the questions that follow.

This week, you have learned about industrialization in America. Today you will choose an invention to research. Find out who invented it, when it was invented, and why people needed it. Use resources such as books, videos, the Internet, etc. as needed. Write a paragraph about it below.

....

....

....

....

....

....

....

....

....

....

....

....

....

....

....

....

IDEAS

problem — thinking — solution

WEEK 17

Economics

Transportation

Learn about the history of transportation in America and how it changed the way people travel.

ARGOPREP

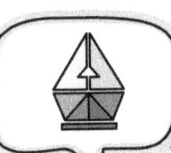
Last week, you learned about industrialization in America. You know that machines made life and work easier for people. This week, you will learn about the history of transportation in America. People made new inventions to help them travel and send items to other places.

Directions: Read the text below. Then answer the questions that follow.

Remember that when Americans started moving West in the 1800s, **wagons** were a popular way to travel. They were pulled by strong animals such as oxen. But wagon trips could take many months to complete and required frequent stops. **Boats** were another option, but they could only be used to travel on water. Americans wanted a better way to travel long distances in a shorter amount of time.

In 1869, the first **transcontinental railroad** was built. People could now use trains for long distance trips across the country. Trips that once took months to complete would now only take a few days. Though railroads had been used for many years, they were designed to travel shorter distances. The transcontinental railroad helped people transport freight items such as fruits, vegetables, and grains from one place to another. By the early 1900s, public trains also became a common form of daily passenger transportation.

1. What were the cons of traveling by wagon?

   A. It could take months to complete one trip.

   B. Wagons could only be ridden on water.

   C. People could not find strong animals to pull the wagon.

   D. Wagons were no longer available in the 1800s.

2. What is a transcontinental railroad?

   A. a train system used for short trips

   B. a wagon that can be used to travel long distances

   C. a train system that allows cross-country travel

   D. all of these

3. True or false?

   Trains became a common way to transport both freight and people.

   A. true

   B. false

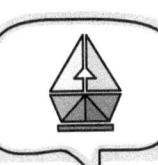
Yesterday you learned how transportation in America began to change in the 19th century. People created faster ways to travel and transport items around the country. Today you will learn about how automobiles, or cars, changed the way people traveled in America.

Directions: Read the text below. Then answer the questions that follow.

Although the first **automobile** was invented in Europe, Americans soon began producing their own. American companies, such as Ford and General Motors, used mass production to make several cars at once. Their efforts eventually led to the rise of the American car industry.

Henry Ford was one of the greatest pioneers in the American automobile industry. In 1903, he founded the Ford Motor Company and hired workers to start making cars. A few years later, he introduced the Model T car. Many people wanted to buy it. Ford had to hire more workers to make more cars at a quicker rate. Eventually, the Ford Motor Company produced nearly 15 million Model Ts. It was now the largest car manufacturer in the world.

Since cars were now widely available, many Americans relied on them to travel both short and long distances. People loved the freedom of having their own form of transportation.

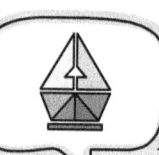
1. How did mass production help the car industry in America?

2. Why do you think people wanted to buy cars instead of using other types of transportation?

"

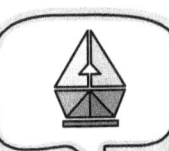
You have learned about how trains and cars changed the way people travel in America. People created new ways to travel by land. Today you will learn about the invention of the airplane.

Directions: Read the text below. Then answer the questions that follow.

Orville and Wilbur Wright had always been fascinated by the idea of flying. As kids, they played with flying toys and hoped that they could someday build a real one. The Wright brothers grew up and started making bicycles. They later opened their own bike shop. The skills they developed led them to create the first **airplane.**

The Wright brothers studied gliders that were already available. These devices could briefly fly but did not have enough power or strength for trips of longer distances. Orville and Wilbur wanted to add engine power to their airplane. In 1903, they built the Wright Flyer I which had a gasoline engine. After weeks of testing and making changes, it flew successfully for 12 seconds! They continued to perfect the airplane over the years. In 1905, they made the Wright Flyer III, which they successfully flew for for 39 minutes and 23 seconds.

The Wright brothers inspired more airplane improvements over the years. People used stronger materials and created space for large groups of passengers. Today, millions of people travel by air.

1. What helped the Wright brothers learn how to build airplanes?

    A. They went to a school for aircraft builders.

    B. They watched videos about building gliders.

    C. They started building bikes and used these skills.

    D. They asked someone to teach them how to build planes.

2. Why couldn't people use gliders to travel?

    A. Gliders could only be used on land.

    B. Gliders were too fast for people to ride on.

    C. Gliders took too long to build.

    D. Gliders were not strong enough to fly long distances.

3. True or false?

The Wright brothers' first airplane flew successfully for almost an hour.

    A. true

    B. false

Directions: Read the text below. Then answer the questions that follow.

You know that transportation in America has changed over the years. Today you will think about the type of transportation that you use.

1. How do you travel to places in your community, like your school?

....

....

....

....

....

2. Have you ever traveled to a place that was far away from home? How did you get there?

....

....

....

....

....

3. How do you think life would be different if there were no trains, cars, planes, etc. in America?

....

....

....

....

....

This week, you have learned about transportation in America. Transportation continues to change over time. People find new ways to improve it. Today you will explore modern transportation and compare it to the transportation of the past.

Directions: Read the text below. Then answer the questions that follow.

Past	Present

1. What kind of changes do you notice between past and present transportation?

....

....

....

2. Why do you think these changes were made?

....

....

....

WEEK 18

Economics
Physical Features

Discover how physical features and structures in America help people travel.

ARGOPREP

*Last week, you learned about the history of transportation in America. As people created new ways to travel, they had to make new **structures**. They also used **physical structures** to travel.*

Directions: Read the text below. Then answer the questions that follow.

A **structure** is something that is built by people. Bridges and railroads are structures, for example. People build them in order to travel more easily. With more cars on the road in America, there was a greater need for roads, highways, etc. People built railroads and subways for train travel.

Although land travel became more popular in the 19th century, people still used water to travel and transport freight. Water travel required physical features such as rivers and lakes. A **physical feature** is something that nature created.

1. What are structures?

   A. things that were created by nature

   B. things that are built by people

   C. things that made transportation more difficult

   D. none of these

2. Which of these is a physical feature that we use to travel?

   A. oceans

   B. rivers

   C. lakes

   D. all of these

3. Why did Americans need to build new structures for transportation?

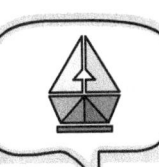
Yesterday you learned how people use structures and physical features to travel. Today you will learn more about specific structures in America.

Directions: Read the text below. Then answer the questions that follow.

Remember that bridges are structures that people use to travel. Cars and freight trucks can be driven over bridges. **Bridges** are built over large bodies of water or land. One of the most popular bridges in America is the **Golden Gate Bridge.** It was built in 1937 because people wanted a quicker way to travel to and from San Francisco. The Golden Gate Bridge was built over San Francisco Bay and the Pacific Ocean. It was now easier to drive across the bridge than travel by boat or ferry.

In many large cities, structures were built for the **public train system.** New York City, for example, constructed a **subway** to allow trains to travel underground. Some rails, called **elevated train systems,** are above ground. The **New York City subway** opened in the 1900s, and millions of passengers still use it today.

1. How did bridges make travel easier for drivers?

   A. People could now drive underground.

   B. People could drive over large bodies of water.

   C. People could drive to other countries.

   D. People were not allowed to drive over bridges.

2. True or false?

   New York City trains can travel both underground and above ground.

   A. true

   B. false

3. Why was the Golden Gate Bridge built?

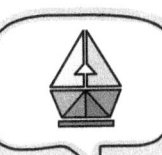
*You know that people use both structures and physical features to travel in America. Today you will learn how **canals** changed water travel.*

Directions: Read the text below. Then answer the questions that follow.

A **canal** is a water system that people have created. It allows boats and ships to travel from one body of water to another. Unlike physical features, such as rivers, canals are not fully created by nature. Workers dig a tunnel in the ground near a body of water to create a stream.

The **Erie Canal** was built in the 1800s to connect the Great Lakes with the Atlantic Ocean. It created a water path from New York City to the Midwest, making it easier to transport items such as food, clothing, and furniture. As a result, New York City became the busiest port in America.

While the Erie Canal was good for transportation, it invaded the homeland of many Native Americans, including the Oneida, Onondaga, Cayuga, Seneca, and Haudenosaunee people. Many Native Americans were removed from this land where the canal was built and sent to reservations.

1. Why was the Erie Canal built?

   A. to connect the Great Lakes with the Atlantic Ocean
   B. to create a water path from New York City to the Midwest
   C. to make transportation easier
   D. all of these reasons

2. True or false?

   A canal is a physical feature that is created by nature.

   A. true
   B. false

3. How did the Erie Canal affect Native American people living on the land where it was built?

You have learned about structures and physical features in America. You know that people can use these structures to travel. Today you will learn more about the structures and physical features where you live.

Directions: Read the text below. Then answer the questions that follow.

Look up information about bridges, canals, rivers etc., in your city and/or state. Write what you learned in the table below.

Structures in my community	Physical features in my community

Today you will review what you have learned about structures and physical features in America this week.

Directions: Read the text below. Then answer the questions that follow.

1. Which of these is a structure?

    A. stream

    B. river

    C. railroad

    D. tree

2. Where is the Golden Gate Bridge?

    A. New York City

    B. San Francisco

    C. Chicago

    D. Washington D.C.

3. What is the New York City subway?

    A. a canal that was built for ships

    B. a bridge that was built for cars

    C. an ocean that was built for boats

    D. an underground structure that was built for trains

4. Explain the pros and cons of the Erie Canal.

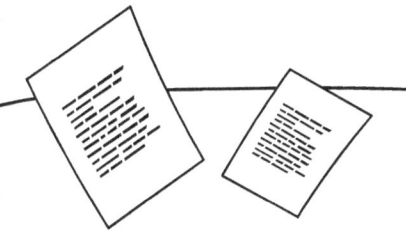

WEEK 19

Economics

The Economy

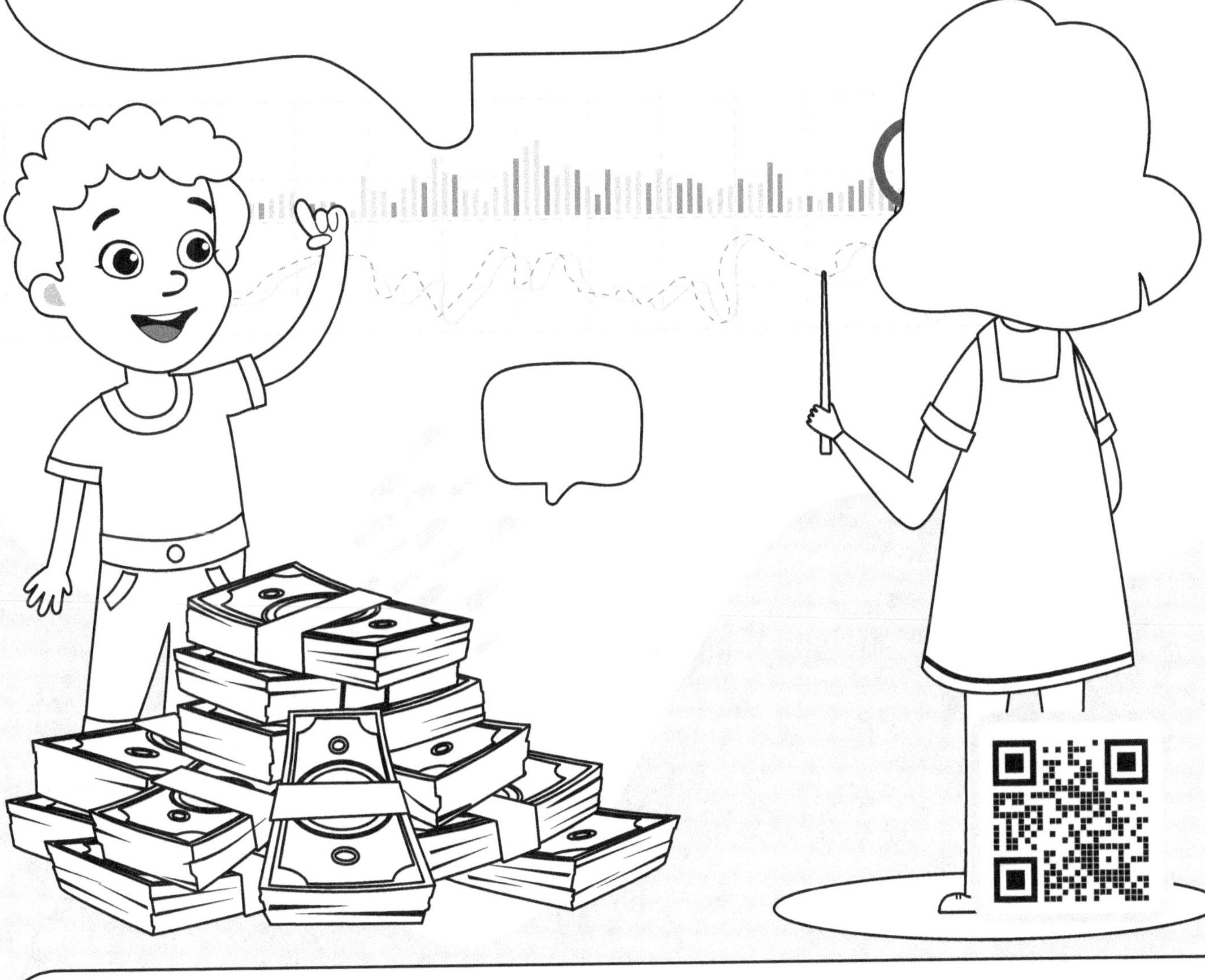

Learn about the economic system in America and explore how people make and spend money.

*You have learned about important topics such as industrialization and transportation in America. You know that over the years, people have created ways to make life easier. These changes also helped people make more money. This week, you will learn more about the American **economy**. An economy is the wealth and resources of a country, as well as the way people make and spend money.*

Directions: Read the text below. Then answer the questions that follow.

Remember that people invented new machines and tools to make work easier. These improvements helped companies make more money. Mass production in industries such as cars, clothing, and food produced millions of dollars for the **American economy.** The introduction of new transportation also helped people sell more products. They could now ship them to other locations in America rather than just selling locally.

1. What is the economy?

    A. the number of people living in a country

    B. the way people make and spend money

    C. the amount of time it takes to travel

    D. the year when a product was invented

2. Which of these factors helped the American economy?

    A. mass production

    B. new inventions

    C. improvements in transportation

    D. all of these

3. True or false?

Although the American economy improved, companies could only sell products in their local communities.

    A. true

    B. false

Yesterday you learned about the American economy. You know that the economy improved as life and work changed in America. Today you will learn more about how this works.

Directions: Read the text below. Then answer the questions that follow.

The economy consists of **producers** and **consumers**. Producers make **goods** or offer **services**. Goods are things that people eat, drink, or use to meet their needs. A service is a job that people do for someone else. Consumers buy these goods and services. As this cycle continues, the money that is made and spent helps the economy.

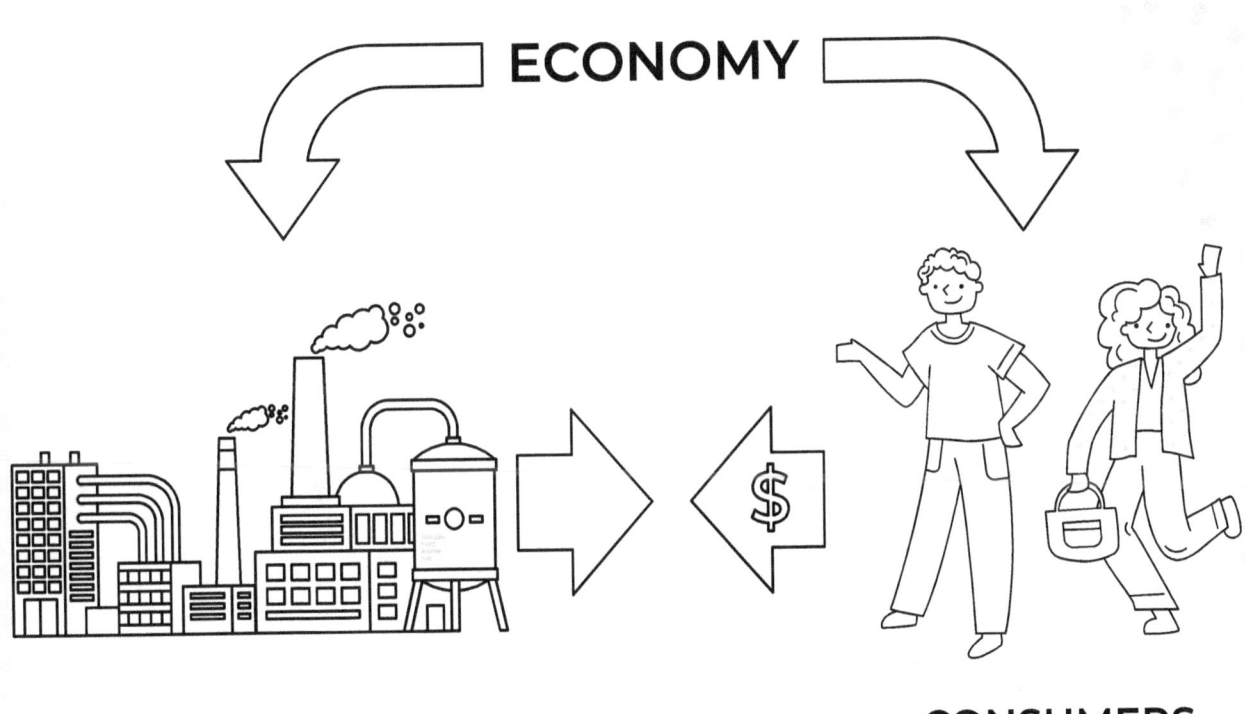

PRODUCERS

CONSUMERS

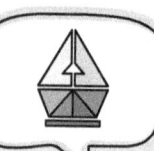
1. Explain in your own words how money is made and spent in the economy.

Yesterday you learned about how the economy works. Producers and consumers create a buying and spending cycle to help the economy. Today you will take a closer look at how America's economy has grown over the years. Certain events in history have led to this growth.

Directions: Read the text below. Then answer the questions that follow.

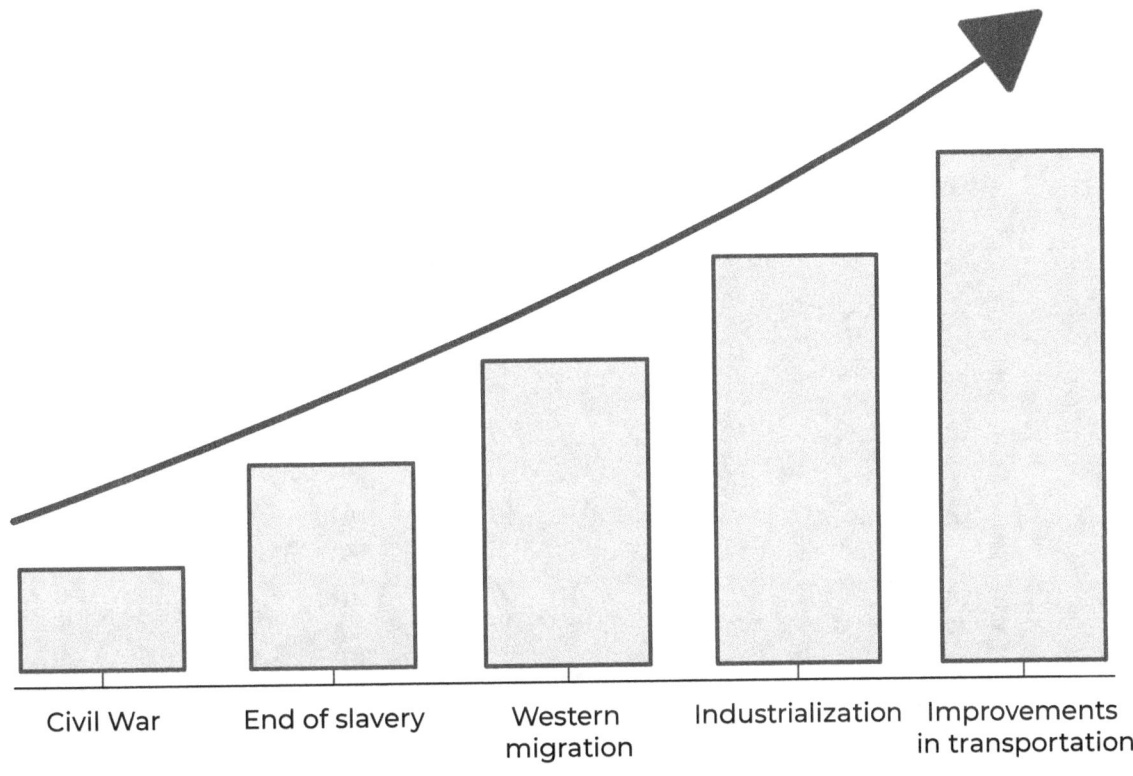

Economic Growth in America

Civil War | End of slavery | Western migration | Industrialization | Improvements in transportation

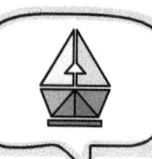
1. Look at the chart. What do you notice about the economy from the 1800's to the 1900s?

2. Did the American economy get better or worse over time? Why do you think this happened?

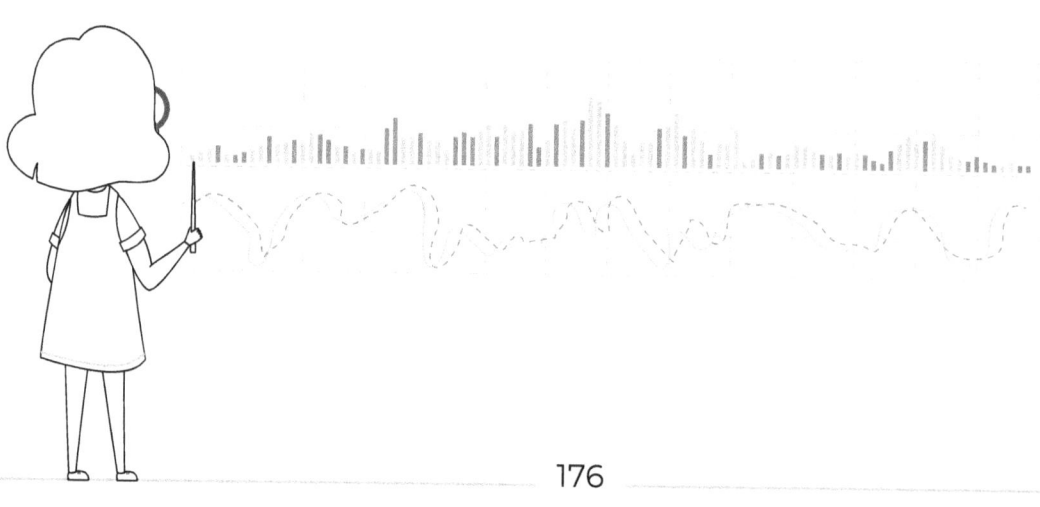

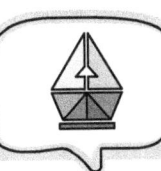
Yesterday you learned more about the American economy. Today you will think about how producers and consumers encouraged economic growth in America.

Directions: Read the text below. Then answer the questions that follow.

You know that producers make goods or offer services. Consumers buy them. Pick a specific industry you have learned about such as automobiles, farming, or clothing. Fill in the information below.

Industry

Who are the producers?

Who are the consumers?

Which goods or services does this industry provide?

This week, you have learned about the American economy. Today you will review what you have learned.

Directions: Read the text below. Then answer the questions that follow.

1. Which of these is NOT part of the economic cycle?

  A. money

  B. goods

  C. laws

  D. consumers

2. What do consumers do?

  A. They make goods and services.

  B. They buy goods and services.

  C. They transport goods and services.

  D. all of these

3. Which of these people is a producer?

  A. a factory worker who makes furniture

  B. someone who is shopping for clothes at the mall

  C. a truck driver who transports food

  D. someone who pays for a delivery service

4. True or false?

  As life improved in the 19th century, the American economy continued to grow.

  A. true

  B. false

WEEK 20

Economics

Immigration

Learn about the reasons why immigration increased in America during the 1800-1900s.

ARGOPREP

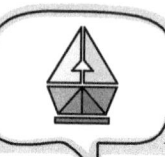
*Last week, you learned about the American economy. You know that it began to improve in the 19th century. As people in other countries watched America grow, they also wanted to achieve similar success. Many people started moving to America. Movement from one country to another is called **immigration**. Today you will learn about the history of immigration in America.*

Directions: Read the text below. Then answer the questions that follow.

   In the late 1800s, nearly 12 million **immigrants** arrived in the United States. They mainly came from European countries such as Germany, Ireland, and England. Like the original American settlers, many of them left their countries to escape government leadership. People had suffered religious persecution, mistreatment from leaders and poor living conditions. Immigrants saw more opportunities for freedom and economic growth by moving to the United States.

1. What is immigration?

   A. when people move from one country to another
   B. when people ship goods to another country
   C. when people live in a country for more than 10 years
   D. when people are unhappy with their country's leader

2. Where did most American immigrants come from in the late 1800s?

   A. China
   B. Africa
   C. Europe
   D. Canada

3. How was immigration in the 1800s similar to American settlement in the 1600-1700s?

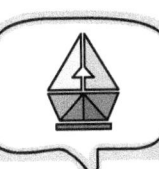
Yesterday you learned about immigration in America. You know that many people started to move to America from other countries in the late 1800s. Today you will learn more about how they came to America.

Directions: Read the text below. Then answer the questions that follow.

> **New York** became known as the "Golden Door," as many immigrants entered America through its ports. Immigrants from Asia arrived on the West coast. But about 70 percent of immigrants arrived on the East coast. In 1892, the American government opened a new immigration station in New York called **Ellis Island.**
>
> Ellis Island has a rich history that is connected to immigration in America. It is now a national landmark that many people visit.

You can take a virtual tour of Ellis Island at https://www.nps.gov/hdp/exhibits/ellis/Ellis_Index.html. Write a paragraph about what you learned from this tour below.

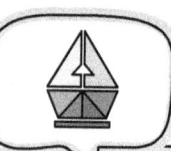
Yesterday you learned about how immigrants came to America. You know that millions of people arrived at Ellis Island. Today you will learn more about their lives as American immigrants.

Directions: Read the text below. Then answer the questions that follow.

"

Remember that people moved to America for many reasons. One of those reasons was to find better jobs. There were many **job opportunities** in factories and other businesses in America. However, many immigrants struggled to find jobs. They had to compete with American citizens who were also looking for jobs. Also, some companies would take advantage of immigrants, giving them more work and less pay. Some people did not want to hire immigrants at all.

Many immigrants faced other challenges as they tried to adjust to life in America. Some did not speak English very well, which caused a **language barrier** between immigrants and English-speaking citizens. It was also difficult to read signs and important documents. To make matters more challenging, some immigrants faced **discrimination** and mistreatment because they were seen as different or strange. These challenges were discouraging to many people who came to America hoping for a better life.

"

1. Why did many immigrants struggle to find jobs in America?

   A. They did not have the skills that they needed to work.
   B. There were very few jobs available in America.
   C. They had to compete with American citizens.
   D. They did now know where to find jobs.

2. True or false?

   Some companies refused to hire immigrants or paid them low wages.

   A. true
   B. false

3. List 3 challenges that immigrants faced in America.

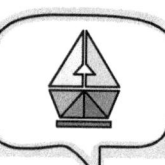
You have learned about immigration in America. Today you will think about your own family history.

Directions: Read the text below. Then answer the questions that follow.

1. What country do you live in? Were you born in this country?

....

....

....

2. Has your family ever lived in another country? Why did they move to a new country?

....

....

....

....

3. What do you know about your family history? Where did they live 100 years ago?

....

....

....

....

....

....

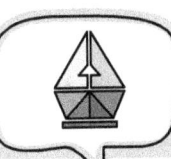
*You know that many immigrants came to America during the 19th century. Many people still move to America from other countries today. They go through a special process to become American citizens called **naturalization**. Today you will learn more about this process.*

Directions: Read the text below. Then answer the questions that follow.

There are **specific requirements** that immigrants must meet to become American citizens. Look at the list below:

Be of the minimum required age (typically, at least 18)

Live in the United States for a certain number of years (must have a **green card** which grants permission to live and work in America)

Establish residency in the state or U.S. Citizenship and Immigration Services (USCIS) district where they plan to live

Have "good moral character"

Be able to speak and write basic English

Have a basic understanding of U.S. history

Register for military service (if male and of a certain age) and be willing to perform civil service when required

Pledge allegiance to the United States

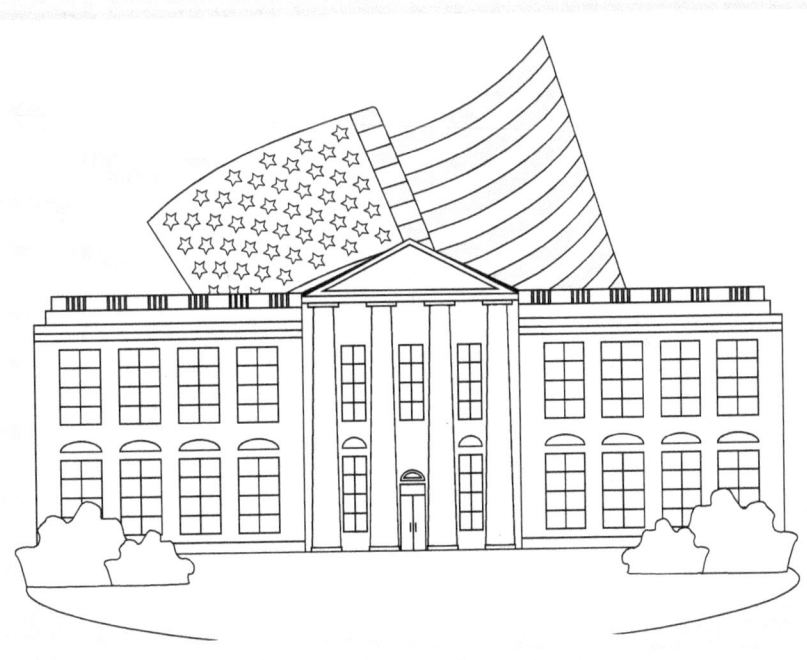

1. Which of these is NOT a requirement for U.S. naturalization?

A. Find a job upon arrival in the United States.

B. Pledge allegiance to the United States

C. Live in the United States for a certain number of years.

D. Have a basic understanding of U.S. history.

2. Why do you think there are requirements to become an American citizen?

....

....

....

....

....

....

....

....

Answer Sheets

To see the answer key to the entire workbook, you can easily download the answer key from our website!

*Due to the high request from parents and teachers, we have removed the answer key from the workbook so you do not need to rip out the answer key while students work on the workbook.

 To watch free video explanations go to: **argoprep.com/social4** OR scan the QR Code:

Place your mouse over the workbook you have, and you will see the "Download Answers" button.

For detailed video instructions on how to access the "Answer Sheets," please scan this QR code.

Books explanations

All Books   Grade: All   Series: Social Studies   Search...

7th Grade Social Studies: Daily Practice Workbook

5th Grade Social Studies: Daily Practice Workbook

8th Grade Social Studies: Daily Practice Workbook

4th Grade Social Studies: Daily Practice Workbook

3rd Grade Social Studies: Daily Practice Workbook

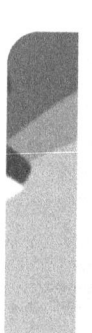

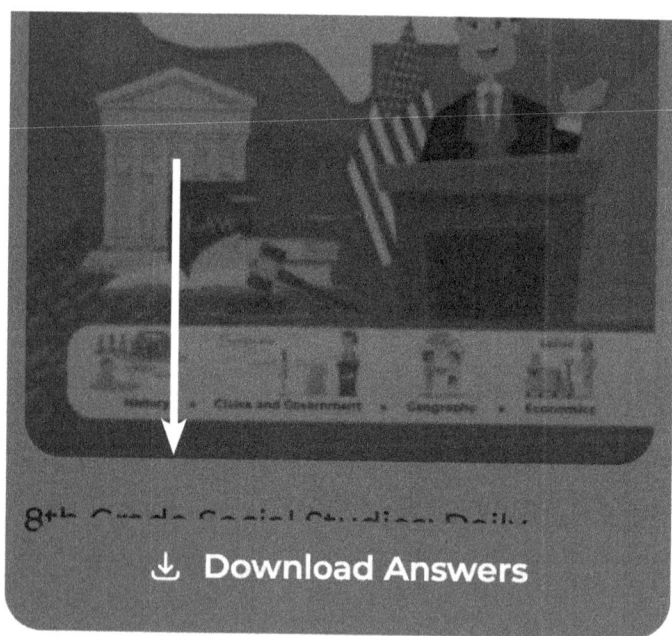

8th Grade Social Studies: Daily

⬇ Download Answers

4th Grade Social Studies: Practice Workbook

www.ingramcontent.com/pod-product-compliance
Lightning Source LLC
Chambersburg PA
CBHW081327120626

46546CB00011B/3253